I want to dive into the rift between the American and Eurasian continents.

I want to surf on the waves where the whales come.

I want a tender and juicy lamb steak cooked on an active volcano.

You're crazy, buddy. Do you think it's possible to do it anywhere?

Realistically speaking, my friend, all these miracles are on one amazing island on Earth and it is only a 5-hour flight from New York.

That's how I heard about this pristine place for the first time.

I've always loved extreme trips, and while it is not a big island, you can find a lot of extreme entertainment. This is a small island between America and Europe, near Greenland and the North Pole.

Here the sky is so close it seems you have become a giant and can reach the clouds. Here, everything is pristine and mysterious. Here the processes of the birth of islands are still taking place just as continents were born here millions of years ago. Iceland. Welcome to the world of an unearthly pristine nature.

On the edge of the inhabited world, near the northern point of the earth's axis, surrounded by eternal ice is the island of Iceland. This is a piece of wildlife, where life is boiling in the truest sense of the word. There are only a few places on the planet, and this island occupies one of the first places rightfully. If you want to visit another planet, but are not ready to fly into space, then you must get to this island. You need not fly to the Moon or Mars. There are 140 volcanoes!

Among them, are a lot of unique natural objects and phenomena: giant glaciers, fields of geysers, frozen lava rivers, volcanic lakes, thermal springs and stunning, beautiful waterfalls!

The planet Earth millions of years ago, when the continents were forming.

Iceland is a world of extraterrestrial landscapes.

This is a new and complete guide.

The guide has been written from a first-person perspective, based on personal experience.

It is a handy and informative guide.

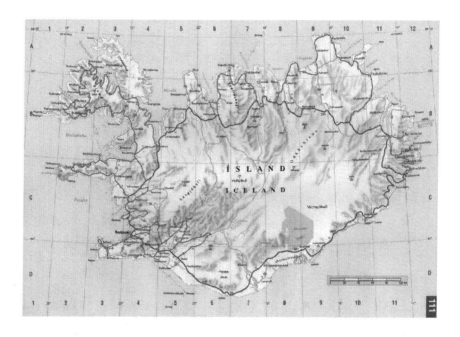

The book includes all the necessary links for easy moving, routes and lots of useful information.

This guide includes the best exciting places where you can spend your vacation in Iceland.

Here you will find essential information for planning your rest.

Attractions include:

Spa Blue Lagoon, Geysers, Waterfalls, Glaciers, National Parks, etc. Fun and interesting places to spend your time. With this guide, you can choose suitable accommodation.

Hotels, shops, night clubs, and many outdoor activities such as:
Whale watching, Diving, Surfing,
Mountain safaris, Ice climbing,
Salmon fishing, Horse riding, etc.

Also here you will find lots of useful information, such as where to buy unlimited 4G Internet across the country. There is the best and most interesting route step-by-step throughout Iceland. This guide includes information on how to reach Iceland, where to stay and weather conditions to help you better plan your trip. You will not have to re-read lots of "guff"; you will find useful facts and specifics.

P.S. I Hope my guide will be useful to you. In this book, you will find many beautiful pictures accompanied by a brief description.

Dear readers, if you want to change, add or you don't like something in my books, please send me e-mail larskkjonsson@gmail.com, and we can talk about it. I'm always glad to meet with my readers. I'm writing for you, and I want to do it better.

Before our trip to Iceland, I want to introduce you to some of the great Icelandic waterfalls.

More information inside the book

Svartifoss waterfall

Godafoss waterfall

Seljalandsfoss waterfall

CONTENT

CHAPTER 1 16

   General facts about Iceland. 16

   Weather in Iceland throughout the Year 18

   What Season Should I Choose for the Trip?............21

   What to Wear...23

CHAPTER 2 26

   How Much Will it Cost to Travel to Iceland?..........26

   How to Get to Iceland 27

   Fly to Iceland 27

   Book Air Tickets...28

   Sail to Iceland 28

CHAPTER 3 30

Where to Stay While Traveling in Iceland 30

   Mobile homes 30

   Camping 31

   Hostels...33

   Farms and Cottages..35

   Guest Houses 37

   Hotels 38

   Apartments in Reykjavik 40

Food 42

CHAPTER 4 47

How to Spend Your Vacation in Iceland.................................47

  Whale Watching..47

  Northern Lights 50

  Geothermal Pools and Spas 52

  Activity in Iceland 56

CHAPTER 5 Capital of Reykjavik 66

  The Sights of Reykjavik..66

    Beach Nautholsvik...66

    Museum of Photography 66

    Lake Ellidavatn 67

    Fjord, Hvalfjordur..68

    Spa Center "Blue Lagoon" 69

    Geysir "Great Geysir." 71

    Peace Tower..75

    Harpa Concert Hall 77

    Zoological Family Park...80

    Mansion Hofdi House...80

    Viking Maritime Museum...81

    Icelandic Phallological Museum 82

Nightlife. Nightclubs and Discos in Reykjavik. 84

Shopping in Reykjavik...88

What to Buy as a Gift in Iceland 89

CHAPTER 6 Tours in Iceland 91

Tour to Whalefjord and Videy Island. 97

Tingvallavatn 100

Volcano Laki or Lakagigar...102

You Can Travel to Iceland by Yourself..........................104

The Photo Tour around the Island and a Trip on Yachts along the
Western Fjords. 105

Day one - 108

Day two 108

Day three...111

Day four..114

Day five 117

Day six 119

Day seven 122

Day eight 125

Day nine 129

Tour around the Island..132

Day one. 132

Day two. 133

Day three..134

Day four...135

Day five. 136

Day six. 137

CHAPTER 7 Helpful information for tourists 139

Visa information..139

Useful phone numbers...139

Mobile & internet in Iceland 140

Save Your Budget in Iceland..141

Photo Survey of Some Icelandic Waterfalls 143

CHAPTER 1

General facts about Iceland.

Travel to Iceland can be compared to a walk on the Moon or Mars, everything here is unusual and fantastic.

Iceland is a large island in the North Atlantic region. The descendants of the Vikings live here, predominantly. This country is the westernmost country in Europe with the northernmost capital of the world.

The first time you see the Icelandic landscape, you can imagine yourself as Neil Armstrong first stepping on the moon – his whole horizon covered with fancy solidified lava, craters, imposing basalt cliffs, and colorful rhyolite mountains. Stone beauty is replaced by wide meadows, reminding many of a scene from *Lord of the Rings* by J.R.R. Tolkien

To complete the picture of Iceland, natural hot mineral water geysers splash up from the ground. Grand waterfalls, fog, and dew beautifully settle on the rocks and grass around the geysers.

A trip to Iceland will allow you to access the world in which people still live, surrounded by wild and beautiful Nordic nature, but their living standard is one of the best in the world.

Pristine, untouched nature will delight you: huge glaciers, volcanoes, powerful waterfalls, and hot springs. The country is rich in traditions - houses of the Icelanders, their music, history all are full of national flavor. This island will give you energy and amazing nature, colorful and vivid, leaving you with an unforgettable experience.

Weather in Iceland throughout the Year

You can visit Iceland in summer and winter, and you will always find many interesting things on this island. The weather here is harsh, but this fresh air is hard to find anywhere else.

Iceland weather in summer in mostly warm and soft. A gentle breeze comes now and again.

Due to volcanic activity, numerous geysers and hot springs, the island is always warming up and the air temperature in the coldest months in winter does not fall below 25-27 ^{0}F (-3 to -4 ^{0}C). In the winter, the air in Iceland becomes even purer and more transparent.

Summer in Iceland

In Iceland, there is daylight 24 hours a day in the second half of May through the end of July. At the end of June in Reykjavik, the sun sinks beneath the horizon for less than 3 hours. Walking at midnight in the city, you can forget about the time and that it's even night. The night-time sky is as bright and blue as the daytime without sunlight.

The hottest summer month is July when average daytime temperatures remain 57-59^{0}F (14-15^{0}C) and night 44-50^{0}F (7-10^{0}C). In summer the weather changes between warm, cool and wet periods. From June to August, Iceland offers the most for travel, as it is the middle of summer here–temperatures reach 68^{0}F (20^{0}C). In August, in Iceland, the average temperature is around 59^{0}F (15^{0}C).

Autumn in Iceland

In October, the weather changes highly, due to cyclones that pass through the Atlantic Ocean.

As for November, this time begins a dark period, when the weather in Iceland in the fall depends on the height of the Sun.

Winter in Iceland

Cold strong wind is common in all of Iceland in December and the dark season comes when daylight lasts more than five hours. The weather in Iceland in winter is mild and windy. The coldest month of the winter season is January. At this time on the coast the temperature during the day is 32-35^{0}F (0-2^{0}C) and at night: 25-27 ^{0}F (–3 –4^{0}C).

Spring in Iceland

Spring off the coast of Iceland accumulates drift ice, which gathers in the winter. In March, in Iceland the temperature remains 35-37^{0}F (2-3^{0}C) and the precipitation decreases. The weather in Iceland in the spring remains snowy. In April and May, in Iceland it will get warmer and temperatures rise to around 44-50^{0}F (7-10^{0}C).

Actual weather in Iceland you can always find on the weather site

http://www.vedur.is

What Season Should I Choose for the Trip?

The most popular season for visiting Iceland is from the middle of June to September when it is hot in European countries. The height of tourist season coincides with June-August, a traditional vacation and leave period in Europe. It is an expensive season.

There are discounts for accommodation rent and tours from September to May.

Autumn dazzles you with its colors and mainly calm weather.

Winter is mild in Iceland, and you can admire the Northern Lights in winter. The daylight lasts only a few hours, there are few tourists, so hotels are cheap.

If your budget is limited, it is best to travel in May-April as many hotels increase their rates almost twice from June 1st.

What to Wear

When choosing your clothing to travel around Iceland, please remember that a good hooded waterproof windbreaker jacket may come useful in any season here. A warm sweater should be taken in summer or winter. When your trip plans include outdoor trips, a warm sweater is especially important.

It is best to choose sportswear for your journey to Iceland. You will feel the most comfortable in such active wear. Also, take hiking shoes along with you.

In planning your trip to Iceland, it is worth remembering that you are going to the north, to the Arctic Circle.

Iceland is a cold North Atlantic country. It has a subarctic climate. Iceland Island extends closely to the Arctic Circle line so that even in high summer it is always cool there and there is little heat. Often, even in the summer, there are some days when it is cold, rainy and extremely windy. You will be walking on gravel during all excursions. Therefore, it is very important to put the right shoes and clothing on, so that the changing Iceland weather will not mar your impressions but add new, bright colors to your trip instead!

You should wear thermal underwear or tights under your trousers and a warm turtleneck sweater under your jacket with a hood; it is a must to wear a woolen hat and woolen (not leather) gloves or mittens.

If it happens to be rainy, waterproof trousers will be helpful. Jeans are not the best thing to wear when it rains as they will absorb moisture and will be drying for several days.

You will need comfortable walking sports shoes, ideally waterproof, and reasonably thick socks, cotton or woolen. Being on tours outside Reykjavik you should not wear high-heeled shoes as you are going to walk on stony surfaces, sand and gravel.

In any season an umbrella is a useless thing in Iceland as it simply gets broken by the Icelandic wind. To keep the rain and wind out, you will need a woolen hat, sweater, and jacket with a hood, anytime, summer included. Then your head will be dry and warm and hands will stay free to take photos.

You can purchase all warm clothing when in Iceland, but shopping will knock you out of the tight schedule of your planned program and will take extra time. Besides, prices for clothing and footwear are much higher in Iceland than in the USA.

The most reasonable way to travel is to take a plane to Iceland, wearing trekking, travel clothing, and put part of it in your luggage. Do not worry about looking weird on the plane. 90% of travelers, flying to Iceland will be dressed the same way: trekking clothing and shoes.

The other 10% are those who have not been warned!

At the same time, there is no dress code in cafes and restaurants in Iceland so you can come to dinner in casual or trekking clothes. Therefore, there is no need to take evening dresses, suits, dress shoes or neck-ties with you.

Sometimes, residents of northern states believe that they know the cold climate well and are not afraid of wind and come to Iceland under cladding (in windbreakers, everyday trousers, without a warm jacket, sweater, hat, and gloves).

However, the chilly north Icelandic wind makes them rush to the nearest clothing shop. The price and climate in Iceland have been mentioned above. Everything is expensive there.

So, here is the conclusion: friends, do not neglect useful tips from this page; wear the right clothing and shoes and your trip to Iceland will go a hundred percent well!

**Hallgrimskirkja Cathedral,
a Lutheran parish church in Reykjavik, Iceland**

CHAPTER 2

How Much Will it Cost to Travel to Iceland?

Regardless of the way you usually take your rest, you may consider three reference variants, although everything is up to each single traveler.

The minimal travel cost starts from 1500 US dollars per person. Suppose there are two people having a ten-day trip to Iceland.

Variant 1: $1500 per person

You book a ticket in advance, having a backpack with a tent on your back. You travel by hitch-hiking or buses, live in camp sites or stay in hostels now and then when the weather is bad, or you need to take a shower; you buy food in grocery stores and cook it on the grill by yourself. This way your expenditures are food and transport, and accommodation from time to time.

Variant 2: $5500 – $6000 per person

You rent a car and drive around the island. You have lunches and dinners in restaurants, stay in 3-4 star hotels, and take several excursion tours.

Variant 3: $15 000 - $17 000 per person

You take a good car, stay at the best hotels and eat at good restaurants. You take tours on helicopters and planes, rent an off-roader and take guides. You will enjoy it all to the fullest.

How to Get to Iceland

You can get to Iceland in two ways, by air and by sea. Flights from the USA will take 4-6 hours. A flight from Europe will take 3-4 hours. Additionally, you can make a short trip to the Atlantic if you choose a tour by ferry.

In Iceland, there are no railways. If you would like to travel to Iceland without a car, you can move easily around the country on buses. The bus service here is well developed.

Fly to Iceland

If you choose air travel, you will arrive at the Keflavik International Airport, also known as Reykjavik-Keflavik Airport (KEF). The airport is located 30 miles (50km) from the capital of Iceland, Reykjavik.

You can stay in Keflavik and start your journey from this city, or you can travel to Reykjavik in a rented car on Road 41, take a taxi or bus transfer.

Bus tickets can be purchased online or may be paid on the spot. In the arrivals hall are located the offices of the major carriers: Airport Express and FlyBus. Buses expect to pick up arriving tourists opposite the exit of the airport. Buses leave 30-40 minutes after the arrival of each new flight.

You can book your transfer from the airport on the airportexpress.is or Flybus *https://www.re.is/flybus* a one-way ticket costs $20-$25. Travel time is 45 min.
The price of a taxi from the airport to Reykjavik is about $120
If you plan to travel to Iceland by bus, buy a bus card, it will save your travel budget.
You also can order a bus card on https://www.straeto.is. Select Shop then General card or click on the direct link https://www.straeto.is/en/verslun/c/alm

Book Air Tickets

You can book tickets for flights on the website of the Icelandic international airlines Icelandair.com
This airline operates flights to Iceland from most American cities.
Also, you can pick and book air tickets from another carrier, for example, Wowair.com, Delta.com, Easyjet.com

Sail to Iceland

Another way to get to Iceland is by ferry from the Danish port of Hirtshals. The ship crosses the Atlantic in 2 days, and a return trip for 2 people with passenger cars will cost approximately $4000 without a meal on board. But this way you can travel around Iceland by car.

You can book your ferry crossing through the online booking engine http://www.smyrilline.com

CHAPTER 3

Where to Stay While Traveling in Iceland

Mobile homes

Iceland is a perfect place for camper fanciers. If you rent a mobile home, you will be able to stop at the most picturesque places on the island. Icelandic camping sites are always clean, and you may enjoy wonderful views. You can fill up your gas tank and replenish your vehicle with water at many filling stations. Moreover, and most importantly, when traveling by mobile home, you will solve the problem of accommodation; you don't need to arrange expensive hotels in advance and you can move at your own pace according to your schedule. You can find more information about camping sites on the Internet; they are paid. You can book a subscription on this website, for example, http://campingcard.is/

Camping

Camping near Alftavatn lake in national park Landmannalaugar. Iceland.

If you choose campsites for an overnight stay in Iceland, you have many choices for accommodation. In Iceland there are about 70 officially registered campsites. Campsites are located along the main road, No. 1, in remote mountainous areas and in the fjords. Campgrounds are open from May to September. The average daily cost per person is $10.The first campground where you can stay http://istay.is/campsite/ is 5 miles from Keflavik international airport to Sandgerdi, southern Peninsula, on Byggdavegur Street, Reykjavik is 35 miles away. If you choose this campground to stop at, remember just 18 miles away is the famous Bluelagoon.com.

Another campsite called T-baer is located in the bay of Herdisarvik, 33 miles from Reykjavik. To reach this campsite from Keflavik international airport, head southeast on 41st Road, then South on 43rd and turn East on Road

427. Near the village of <u>Vik</u>, you'll be able to settle in <u>Vikcamping.is</u> which takes guests from June until late September.

In the East of Iceland, you can stay at a campsite in <u>Mjoifjordur</u>. The eastern fjords are very beautiful, and you will be able to travel the East Coast quite a lot of time, there is always something to see and to do.

<u>Lonsa.is</u> a comfortable camping place outside of <u>Akureyri</u>.

All campsites close at the end of September.

**Landmannalaugar Camping,
Fjallabak Nature Reserve, Central Iceland**

Hostels

In Iceland's capital, you can stay in Reykjavik city hostel http://www.hostel.is

Two, three and six-bedded rooms each have a shower. This hostel has a comfortable courtyard with a garden.

Free Internet access, equipped kitchen and laundry facilities are available, everything you need. You are free to store your luggage and make use of household appliances and a computer.

The reception is open 24 hours.

Nearby there is located a 24-hour supermarket.

In the village of Vik is a cozy hostel, which offers a wonderful view. Everything you need is here. Here is beautiful nature, the south shore and a large, black beach. Here is a nice quiet place to rest where tourists like hiking.

Nearby you can play golf, go horse riding or boating in the sea.

Hofn is a small town with three sides washed by the sea and the fourth side is covered by the largest glacier Vatnajokull.

The hostel here is located in the city center, and everything you need is at your fingertips.

Staying in Hofn you will always find something to do-boat tours, glacier walks on horses, snowmobiles or jeeps. You will not be bored here.

In the east of Iceland, you can stay in the town of Seydisfjordur

The Hostel in Seydisfjordur is located in a former harbor, and the reception is next to the old hospital building. Both buildings have a long history and have not long been renovated. The hostel is located just a few hundred yards from the center. Cozy two–six bedded rooms are decorated with antique furniture and offer beautiful views of the fjord the hostel overlooks.

Internet connection and home appliances are available at this hostel. You will always be happy here.

In the northern capital of Iceland, the city of Akureyri's hostel is located in the city center. This hostel has been owned by the same family for over 50 years. It has a common room, kitchen and dining room. There are cozy hostel rooms with bathrooms and shower. Also, there is a separate cottage with full amenities. In Akureyri, you will find many interesting tours such whale watching, or skiing on the glacier, for example.

Farms and Cottages

**Typical small houses in Iceland.
The are old architecture with a green roof.**

There is an association in Iceland called Icelandic Farm Holidays, www.heyiceland.is It brings together a hundred and a half farmers who offer tourist accommodation in their houses, guest homes or specially equipped hotels. Most of them are located along Road No1 around the whole island.

You'll find three classes of farms there.

Rooms of class I are simple, the shower and WC are for communal use.

Rooms of class II are equipped with wash stands.

Rooms of class III are well-equipped and fitted up with all conveniences.

Private country hotels are marked as class IV and offer comfortable and well-equipped rooms.

Regardless of the room class, all tourists are offered breakfast.

Depending on the farm activity and location, you can ride horses or bicycles, fish or sail a boat, make short trips or play different games, golf included.

You can book a voucher on the association website for the selected number of days, which allows you to travel freely according to your individually planned route and bed down for the night at any nearest farm, being a member of the association. Nevertheless, in summer, in high season, it is best to make a booking beforehand. Prices for farms and cottages depend on their class and start from €50 per room. A nice farm won't costs less than a hotel room, but a farm is exotic.

Guest Houses

Choose a guest house or hotel for more comfort.

For tourists there are many comfortable guesthouses in Iceland. This is a cozy home that costs less than a hotel and sometimes has only one or two rooms available for use. Often a guest house is managed by an Icelandic family. Therefore, you will be taken maximum care of. In the guest house, there are all the amenities, shower, food, and internet. In most guest houses you will be served a tasty breakfast.

Some excellent guest houses in Iceland:

Guest House in Akureyri   http://www.skjaldarvik.is
Guest House in Egilsstadir   www.eyjolfsstadir.is
Guest House in Hofn   http://houseonthehill.is
Guest House in Vik   http://www.likevik.is
Guest House in Reykjavik   http://lily.is

Hotels

The first thing you should get used to is that everything is costly in Iceland. Hotel rooms are no exception; on average, you'll pay twice more than on the continent. One more peculiarity of Iceland is that prices of hotels are in most cases set per person, not per room. So, if you see the room rated €100, you may pay €200 per two people.

It is best to book the hotel beforehand. There are lots of tourists in Iceland, and some hotels have limited availability. Many hotels are closed in winter, but, at the same time, the rest of them reduce their prices by several times.

Keep in mind that it is almost impossible to find five-star hotels outside Reykjavik, and four-stars do not always match their class. On average, a 3–4 star hotel room per 2 people costs €160–200 per night.

There are exciting hotels in Iceland. Ranga hotel, for example, www.hotelranga.is in the small city of Sudurlandsvegur was called "the world's best place to watch polar lights" by the *Sunday Times*. Polar lights are the main amusement here. The best time to watch this natural phenomenon is from September to April.

The network of hotels "Edda" includes 11 hotels located around the coast of Iceland (the route of the Golden Ring).
Hotels can offer you many different services such as:
Rental of transport, open pools with thermal water, conference rooms, restaurants, geothermal baths, kayaks and pleasure boats, various excursions, fishing, golf, horse riding, gyms, also whale watching and birds in their natural

environment and, of course, not forgetting the magnificent landscapes.

Also, "Edda" network hotels host various events like The Great Fish Day or music concerts.

By staying in a hotel Edda, you will be satisfied with your holiday and get a lot of impressions.

Apartments in Reykjavik

The tourist flow to Iceland increases from one year to the next, especially in summer time. Rooms at hotels are booked far in advance, in autumn, winter and spring. It often happens that it is impossible to find a vacant room for reasonable price. Therefore, we advise you to take care of booking your rooms. You will not find it difficult to choose the right variant of accommodation.

Reykjavik and its satellite cities, Kopavogur, Hafnarfjordur, and Mosfellsbaer, have a large number of hotels, guest houses, and hostels. Levels of comfort and prices are ranged from VIP to economy class. Winter prices (from the beginning of October to the beginning of May) are on average 20–30% lower than summer ones (from June 1st to late September). Early booking will give you good chances of getting a discount.

All hotels in Reykjavik and Iceland have a high standard of service and cleanliness and English-speaking personnel.

Large numbers of hotels have rooms of different comfort levels. Guest houses are usually equipped with shared baths and shared kitchens for the guests, but there are also rooms with private bathrooms. Pay attention to the details of each room in the amenities description.

I recommend staying at a hotel in the historic part of Reykjavik; there are many hotels and guest houses on Laugavegur Street. All hotels in the historical part of Reykjavik have zip code 101 Reykjavik.

If there is a 105 Reykjavik zip code in the address name, then the hotel is located not far from Laugavegur Street, yet in that part of it that is somewhat remote from the historical center, and you'll have to walk about 20–40 minutes to reach it. Region 105 Reykjavik is also suitable for tourist accommodation.

Pay attention to the address and postal code and you will not be misled while choosing the location of your hotel in Reykjavik.

It is very comfortable to put up in the central part of Reykjavik. In such case, you will not need any public transport to leisurely walk along the oceanfront and central streets of the capital when you have no excursions.

All exciting museums are densely located in the central part of the capital. There are dozens of stores, cozy cafes, and colorful restaurants in the center.

A good alternative to renting a hotel room is renting an apartment. There is the most homelike atmosphere in apartments. Also, apartments are more spacious. Apartments are well-equipped, including a kitchen and bathroom. The hospitable and friendly residents of Reykjavik offer a wide range of apartments in different city districts.

Food

In Iceland, you won't find many cafes and restaurants. Prices are quite high. Dinner at a restaurant will cost you about €50 per person. A buffet dinner (cold table) at most restaurants will cost you around €30. Junk food can only be found in the capital area. You can find soup, cakes, and sandwiches in any café.

There is a wide variety of sweet courses in Iceland; admirable cakes are baked in almost each cafe.

You can buy amazing vinegar-pickled meats at almost each supermarket or filling station. In Iceland, you will taste the most delicious meat ever! There is delicious and juicy lamb in Iceland. To roast the meat by yourself, you can buy single use roaster (grill). Such roasters can be found at filling stations and in many stores.

During your countryside tour, you can buy some dried fish (hardfiskur) at the nearest filling station to have a snack on your way. That will make your trip much more pleasant, and you will feel like a real Icelander. Many people like dried fish, some get scared away by its smell, but it is worth tasting.

What is worth tasting among national and traditional dishes?

"Lamb on the bone" is quite good and other lamb dishes should be tried without a doubt. Try rye pancakes (flatkaka) with smoked lamb (hangikjot).

Smoked salmon (lax) with rye-bread (rugbraud) is well-liked here. Other popular sandwich ingredients are marinated herring, sausage rolls, and lamb paste.

In Iceland there are many delicious fish. Fish soup is prepared in many places. If you love seafood, this will be delicious for you. There are sea soups, fried fish, seafood salads, fish sandwiches and more. Enjoy it in local restaurants.

Locals bake "volcano" bread in Iceland. Kneaded dough is placed in a metal container and left on the ground in active volcanic regions to bake it. Then a ready loaf of bread is taken out of it. A dairy dish "skir" is usually served as a dessert with strawberries, jam, ice-cream, fruits or whipped cream.

A casual drink in Iceland is coffee. In coffee houses you pay for the first cup only, the rest comes for free. For 75 years, until 1989, beer was totally forbidden in Iceland. Icelandic vodka "Brennivin" is a beverage made of potato and flavored with caraway. There is a wide choice of European alcohol and wines available.

Among Iceland's exotic dishes, you may order whale meat soaked in milk. I suggest you ask the waiter about their fish daily special. For dinner, order special stewed black polar partridge. The meat is black, a bit coarse, but tastes delicious with red berry sauce!

It is very common in Iceland to combine sweet and salty ingredients. Can you imagine, for instance, herring in a honey sauce?

From ancient times they have dried and smoked meat and dished it up as starters.

Exotica lovers may prove themselves by trying a particularly condimental and odorous Icelandic starter – the unforgettable "fermented" shark.

CHAPTER 4

How to Spend Your Vacation in Iceland

Whale Watching

Around the coast of Iceland, it is often possible to meet and observe some of the largest mammals in the world: whales, sharks, sperm whales, blue whales and many other inhabitants of the Atlantic Ocean.

One of the favorite pastimes of tourists in Iceland is <u>whale watching</u>. If you are interested, go to the north of the country—that is the best place for a meeting with the ocean's residents.

In the north, on the Bay of Skjalfandi, is the small and very charming town of Husavik, which is the largest center of whale watching in Europe.

"Whaaaale!" shouted the captain, pointing to the front. With delight and anticipation, run to the board and see the fountain of the whale. This fountain gushes out water at 16–33 yards from you, and you imagine the animal 40–45 ft. in length, slowly moving under the water.

Suddenly, the captain shouts, "He's diving!"

The whale flexes and arches its back, raising its huge tail, and disappears again, plunging into the depths. All accompanied by the enthusiastic cries of the children, clicking cameras and applause of the international public.

Whales spark emotional reactions in just about everyone. Mostly it is because the whales have become a metaphor for the natural balance on Earth. Sperm whales are superior to all the world's mammals in diving. They can dive to a depth of 328 yards, so you are unlikely to see the same whale twice in one trip. But, the chance of seeing several whales is very large, as safaris are arranged in areas rich in fish, plankton, and crustaceans. Here thousands of whales come to feed.

In the summer you can often see sperm whales, but, if you are lucky, you can also look at toothed whales, sharks, blue whales, moor whales, humpback whales, dolphins, and orcas. In addition, on a whale safari you will take in the amazing scenery of Iceland, the abundance of fresh sea air and beauty that will long stay with you!

Duration: 3–3.5 hours

https://www.gentlegiants.is

Northern Lights

Tours for those wishing to experience the <u>Northern lights</u> in Iceland begin in October. One of the most interesting programs is offered in the southern part of the country. First, tourists are taken to the town of Stokkseyri where there are many stories about elves and ghosts. There is an Icelandic Wonders Center and Icelandic wonders dedicated to elves, trolls, and the Northern lights.

In the "winter" part of the Icelandic Wonders Center, which is maintained at subzero temperatures, watching a movie about the Northern lights, tourists are offered the chance to enjoy a drink of ice, which is gouged out Europe's largest glacier, Vatnajokull. Then tourists are taken to Draugasetrid ("Center of ghosts"), where they are told 24 scary stories. After that begins the hunt for the Northern lights.

Conscientious travel agencies arrange tours of the Northern lights with professional "hunters". Best of all it is a unique natural phenomenon that can be seen in the period from 22:00 to midnight. Thus, while tourists enjoy an evening cultural program and refreshments, a professional "hunter" rides in the surrounding area looking for the best place to observe the Northern lights. Only after the lights have been found does the "hunter" call the whole group to the specified place.

The Northern lights are a phenomenon that has attracted and amazed people for centuries. Celestial patterns, changing every second, in fact, are only the result of the collision of the solar wind with the Earth's atmosphere. This process goes on continuously. Theoretically, the Northern lights occur year round; however, they are not always visible. The best place to observe this miracle of nature is the Arctic, but the best time is from October to March, this is the darkest time of the year and it is, therefore, more likely that you will see the Northern lights. Besides the darkness, it is also important that the sky is clear: even a small cloud will prevent the clear glow of the Northern Lights.

Geothermal Pools and Spas

The geothermal Blue Lagoon, formed around a set of natural pools, is one of the most popular natural attractions in Iceland. Every year the resort is visited by almost 300 thousand people. The first bathing area appeared in the Blue lagoon in the mid-80s of the last century. Hot springs, sky blue, baby blue and milk shades are washed by the lava piles, creating contrasting landscapes.

Since 1976, the volcanic origin complex has been known to have unique therapeutic and healing properties. Minerals, sea salt, sulfur and blue-green algae in the water can cure skin diseases. You can swim here even in winter. Water in deep tanks throughout the year retains a comfortable temperature from +37° to +40°C, about 100 Fahrenheit.

WORKING HOURS

The Blue Lagoon is open daily throughout the year. Working hours

In June: from 9:00 to 21:00;
From July 1 to August 15: from 9:00 to midnight;
From August 16 to 30: from 9:00 to 21:00
From September 1 to May 31: from 10:00 to 20:00.

With the exception of Christmas and New Year holidays; during the period from 23 December to 1 January, the schedule should be specified on the <u>Bluelagoon official site</u> Bluelagoon.com. Guests can stay in the thermal complex for 45 minutes after closing.

THE COST OF ATTENDING

The price of admission depends on the season. From September 1 to May 31 the cost of visiting the Blue Lagoon is 33 euros for adults, 15 euros for teenagers 14 and 15 years. From 1 June to 31 August entrance for adults will cost 40 euros, 15 euros for teenagers 14 and 15 years. For children under 13, entry is free when accompanied by adults.

More information about the cost of cosmetic procedures, as well as rental of bathrobes and towels, can be found on the <u>website of Blue Lagoon.</u>

TIPS

All visitors to the Blue Lagoon resort will receive a bracelet with a magnetic chip that is the key to a personal locker. You need to bring a swimsuit; towels and bathrobes can be rented for an additional fee. Locker rooms are divided into male and female areas. There are showers (shampoo and shower gel are provided free of charge). Also, a bracelet with a chip is used to pay for snacks and drinks in the bar and restaurant, at the thermal baths so money and other things are best left in your locker.

To visit the Blue lagoon special shoes are not required.

The water in the pools is renewed every two days.

The Blue Lagoon website has a special section where you can consult or ask a question about the features of the resort.

HOW TO GET THERE

The geothermal Blue Lagoon is located 23.6 miles to the southwest of Reykjavik; travel time from the capital bus station is 45 minutes. Keflavik International Airport is located 9.3 miles northwest of the Blue Lagoon. Travel time is about twenty minutes. Buses run between Reykjavik, the airport and thermal baths several times a day throughout the year.

The resort has free lockers where you can leave suitcases and bags.

LOCATION

The geothermal Blue Lagoon is on the Reykjanes Peninsula in southwest Iceland. GPS 63°52'53.4" N22°27'10.1"W

Activity in Iceland

Caves in Iceland can found at every step. A small entrance on the surface often results in massive caves.

The crystal-clear
icy waters around
Iceland will amaze you

Enjoy an exciting
sight born of the
earth's crust on
a fault The Mid -
Atlantic Ridge.

In the mountains of Iceland,
you will find great routes for every taste.
From short walks to multi-day hikes.
You will see sharp mountain peaks,
shining snow caps and barren plains
which sloping down to the shore.

Icelandic horses are obedient, easy to ride.
Tours on lava fields cross the rivers
go among volcanoes, lead you to a great
nature and each second give you
the opportunity to enjoy picturesque
views of this beautiful country.

Some tours are made up for people with
little or no experience in horse riding.
Another specially arranged for experienced riders.

Enjoy the extraordinary
beauty and magnificent
scenery of the ice caves.

The Ice Caves has changed every year,
and every ice cave is unique
and every year has a new form.

The Glaciers are constantly melting and moving, everyday changing their shape, but you will always find a vertical wall of ice.

Tour operators offer full year trips for ice climbers of all skill levels.

Icelandic clear waters ideal for kayaking
and rafting on quiet secluded fjords
this is an excellent pleasure.

Iceland kayaking
suits for you, if not afraid of ice water.
And if you're bored of the simple rapids
overcoming, you can always try out rafting.

Icelandic rivers are rich in salmon and other North fish.

So the most famous fishermen are happy to come to Iceland to throw their fishing rods.

The snowmobile is a kind of alternative to Hiking. Less energy, but just as exciting way to experience the Icelandic glaciers and snow fields.

In recent years Iceland has gained a reputation as one of the best places for surfing.

Though the low water temperature, you can conquer the great waves here. You just need especially a tight suit.

CHAPTER 5 Capital of Reykjavik

The Sights of Reykjavik

Beach Nautholsvik

Guests of Reykjavik have long appreciated the yacht club "Siglunes" and the geothermal beach in Nautholsvik.

The high mineralization of geothermal water helps to get rid of many chronic diseases and enhances immunity.

On site: service center with locker rooms, showers, hot baths and a wide selection of beverages. The optimum temperature of the seawater lagoon is holding at 15–19°C /60–65⁰F; the bath is brought to 30–39°C/85–100⁰F.

Yacht club "Siglunes" is located on the east side of the geothermal beach, which gives children the opportunity to spend unforgettable sailing holidays.

In contrast to the comfortable spa centers, beach Nautholsvik is in a public place, and therefore sometimes crowded. This is not surprising because the view is stunning and, plus, this is probably the only place where you can really "touch" the boundary between the hot thermal water and the freezing breath of the ocean.

Museum of Photography

Five million items were collected at the photography Museum of Reykjavik. In this unique archive are the various collections of photos taken by both professionals and amateurs. The oldest photo is dated 1870.

Topics vary from cute family pictures to industrial landscapes and the whole history of Iceland: its customs and way of life, traditions, industrial development, fashion, advertising, and natural beauty. There are pictures that are forever kept in memory of the wonders of the world that have disappeared under the onslaught of civilization. Exhibitions are regularly changed and updated.

Very original entertainment is offered in the Museum of Photography for young visitors. It is a space for games and a small exhibition of photographs at the same time. Children can feel inside the camera, touch everything inside this mysterious chamber, to see how it turns out.

Lake Ellidavatn

In Reykjavik even being in the capital you will not be divorced from nature; this is one of the greatest advantages of Reykjavik. Lake Ellidavatn is just a 15-minute drive from the city center and is a fantastic way to dive into the past.

Ellidavatn is popular not just for excellent fishing but also its good climate, which positively influences health. There is a lake full of fish, silver trout and fat salmon.

Fishing is permitted daily from 7 am to midnight, and the season for fans to sit with a fishing rod begins with the first day of summer and ends on September 15. It is an especially popular lake in late May – early June and the best chance to pick up trout on the hook is close to the evening or early morning. Fishermen are always welcome here; however, the rules are strict, the population of the valuable fish is under special control.

Large penalties are incurred for abandoning garbage on the shore; you must ride only on the strictly paved route; navigation is prohibited without special permission. Moreover, all anglers must write a report on their catch on a special website.

Fjord, Hvalfjordur

Once out of Reykjavik and past the adjacent town of Mosfellsbaer, the circular road will lead you to the north and the towering mountain of ash. <u>This Fjord, Hvalfjordur,</u> means "whale fjord." The biggest in southwest Iceland, it is named after the huge number of whales there, the legends of which go to the times of the first settlers.

In this area, there are many interesting tourist routes. One of them is in <u>Thingvellir national Park.</u>
<u>Fjord Hvalfjordur</u> has always been one of the main whaling stations in Iceland.

The water of the fjord teeming with fish, here are the main migration routes of herring and a river full of salmon.

Spa Center "Blue Lagoon"

Blue lagoon Iceland is a dream for everyone who wants not just to relax but feel renewed and emerged, in the truest sense of the word, from a geothermal source. This spa is the most visited attraction in Iceland today. The resort is located in the southwest of the country, in Grindavik, 40

minutes' drive from Reykjavik and a short distance from Keflavik Airport.

The main treatment in the "Blue Lagoon" is carried out by using mineral water, which is very rich in beneficial substances, in its composition of silica and sulfur. The waters of the lagoon are renewed every two days, due to the plant's geothermal energy. The services that are offered are unique; there are few centers in the world that have such a generous natural base. For the services of visitors there is a medical center and a beauty salon. You can choose everything that your heart desires. It can be a relaxing massage using special oil with active minerals. The skin becomes healthy and glowing.

The composition of the scrub local cooked silica, resurfaces the skin, removes dead cells and stimulates circulation. All cosmetics used in the "Blue Lagoon" spa are prepared based on the geothermal seawater, minerals, and algae. Cosmetics with such a composition can be found only in Iceland. Treatments with algae are very popular amongst the guests of the center. Professionals can polish the skin with special body wraps. Developed in the Blue Lagoon, the whole system is the strengthening of procedures for pregnant women that relieves swelling and pain in the back.

Beauty—it's true care for the face and body. Special cream and massage make the skin more elastic and visibly reduce the signs of aging. Facials are divided into three categories, each designed for different skin types. For mature skin, they are directed to their own production of collagen and provide essential moisture. For normal and dry, it's first and foremost the strengthening of the protective barrier. Dry and mixed skin is subjected to deep purification and detoxification. There's a very effective silica based deep cleansing mask.

Also available in the spa center is a VIP-service. There is an exclusive interior, which implies privacy and quiet. This complex is designed for 12 people maximum. The living room with fireplace and designer furniture, is an oasis separated from the bustle. Direct individual access to the therapeutic waters of the lagoon is provided for guests. In addition to relaxing spa treatments, guests await an exciting excursion. Experienced guides tell the history of the resort and the natural features of this place, and its value from the point of view of medical science. Everyone can visit the lava fields that stretched near to the spa and learn a lot about volcanic activity in Iceland. The tour necessarily includes local myths about elves and trolls, as well as an original cocktail, the "Blue Lagoon", a visit to the laboratories and a little surprise.

Geysir "Great Geysir."

The "Golden ring" route is the famous Valley of Geysers. Among a dozen large and small sources guides pay attention to the oldest and most famous of them the Great Geysir. It received its name in the mid-thirteenth century from the Icelandic word "geyser", which means "to break", and it gave the name to all other hot springs in the world.

Great Geysir was born after the earthquake in 1294. As a result of the cracking of the earth's crust the hot springs under the ground opened. With a hiss escaping to the outside, they began to gush to a height of about 70 meters. The spectacle is quite fascinating and still attracts crowds of tourists. This geyser wakes up and dies down periodically, and always it is associated with volcanic activity. The diameter of the Geysir is about 3 meters. It's a huge bowl, composed of small limestone rock. During the eruption, it throws up about 230 tons of water!

THE HISTORY OF THE GEYSER

There's a history of the well-preserved facts covering Geysir's life over the last two centuries. In 1894, a local farmer who owned the land in the Valley of Geysers sold it to businessman James Kreiger (by the way, later he became head of the Northern Ireland government). The new owner fenced it off and charged an entrance fee. Sometime later, he gave (!) this unique area to his friend.

In 1935, one of the descendants of the owner sold the land with geysers to Sigurdur Jonasson. Driven by the best motives, that made the area a national treasure and made entrance free. But as we all know, "The road to hell is paved with good intentions." Thanks to the free access to the natural wonder, some cultureless people thought it would be very interesting to throw rocks and dried dirt into a geyser. The spouting of the geyser was ended.

It was necessary to save this important touristic area. At the governmental level a decision was made to create an artificial canal around the geyser, to force it to work. But these measures gave short-term effect. Currently, the canals are artificially washed before the main holiday of Iceland—the Day of National Independence. In 2000, there was a huge earthquake in Iceland. Obviously, the channels of the main geyser were cleaned in a natural way.

The geyser has been operated again in active mode: the eruption took place up to 8 times a day. However, the water fountain was low. But this activity has also gone into recession after three years. Now the Great Geysir "wakes up" rarely, spouting not more than 10 meters. Its main condition is a tranquil lake of turquoise color with a smell of hydrogen sulfide. In the Valley of Geysers is a well-developed infrastructure for many tourists. There's a hotel, café, and restaurant, and a souvenir shop in which you can buy models of geysers, utensils and summer clothes with the geyser's image.

There are stamps and commemorative coins on which are emblazoned the Great Geysir. The guards keep order in the tourist groups. The eruption of thermal springs is associated with the high-temperature water. If you do not follow precautions, you can get burned. By the way, a lot of unwary animals fall in and are cooked alive. But there are swimming areas where the water isn't hot.

By the way, Reykjavik is heated by hot spring water. Due to the cheapness of this fuel, the Icelanders can afford to grow exotic flowers, fruit, and vegetables in numerous greenhouses.

Peace Tower

On Videy Island in Iceland is located a place called <u>the Peace Tower.</u> This tower brings wisdom, healing, and joy. The light beam penetrates the heavens—it's meant to show peace and love, the primary things that bind and sustain life on Earth. Peace Tower also called the Tower of Light; it's a memorial to John Lennon, built by his widow Yoko Ono in 2007. It is huge, 17 meters (about 18 yards) in diameter, and sits on a pedestal of white stone.

On it are inscribed the famous words from the song "Imagine" in approximately 24 languages. The tower is an illusion, created by bright beams of light directed into the sky. The light rays shine out of the cylinders, embedded in a stone base. When the weather is clear, the height of the rays can be up to 4 kilometers (2.5 miles).

The building of Peace Tower started on 9 October 2007, the birthday of the famous musician. One year later, the first ray of light illuminated the heavens. Yoko has developed the design of the tower by herself. At the opening, she said that this tower was the embodiment of her and her husband's shared dreams. "I chose Iceland because the Peace Tower should stand in a unique clean place. Every time I visit this place, it makes me feel 10 years younger. This is actually an answer to prayer for me because the first time John has put forward this idea at home, in England, in the 1966 year. John didn't know how to realize this project and was intend to build a lighthouse in his garden. I waited a long time while we built of Peace Tower".

The tower on the Island of Videy should remind people that the world needs to be protected because the tower and all the inscriptions on the pedestal are a reminder of the peace hymn written by John Lennon—"Imagine". Iceland is difficult to surprise with a light show. This country has numerous volcanic eruptions and the bright flashes of the Northern lights.

However, in this enlightened country I've never seen anything that would compete with the brilliant trace of light that the penetrated the darkness of the Arctic on the night of October 9, at night, when John Lennon would have turned 67 years old. In the presence of 200 people, including Yoko Ono, Sean Lennon (John's son), Ringo Starr, Olivia, widow of George Harrison, and prominent companions of the Dalai Lama, together with the civilian leaders of the city of Reykjavik, the Tower of Peace was turned on for the first time.

The light, on Videy Island, is switched on October 9, John Lennon's birthday, and is lit until 8 December, the date when he was murdered. On this day, the lights go out. Also, floodlights shine on special occasions. The tower is illuminated for the winter solstice (21st to 28th December), New Year's Eve (31 December) and the first week of the Icelandic spring (from 21 to 28 March). It lights up after sunset, two hours before midnight.

Harpa Concert Hall

Concert hall Harpa in Reykjavik's harbor is the most beautiful place in Iceland for concerts, business meetings, large conferences, banquets, and exhibitions. Its vivid facade was designed by renowned artist and architect Olafur Eliasson. He drew inspiration from crystallizing basalt columns commonly found in Icelandic nature.

Only a 3 hour flight from London and 5 hours from New York, the strategic geographical position of Iceland, right in the middle of transatlantic routes, makes it an optimal place for meetings on neutral territory. Business and creative teams arriving from Europe or North America are, always glad to choose exotic Iceland, a country with one of the fastest growing tourism sectors. And the most important meetings are always held in Harpa Hall.

The solid glass wall of the facade changes color depending on the movement of the sun and weather changes.

In 2011, the concert hall became the permanent home for the Icelandic Symphony Orchestra. They give up to 60 concerts each season. Many of the most famous musicians in the world come from this team, including Daniel Barenboim, Anne-Sophie Mutter, Joshua Bell, Hilary Hahn, Mstislav Rostropovich, Radu Lupu, Claudio Arrau, and Evelyn Glennie.

Zoological Family Park

On 22 April, 1986, the City Council of Reykjavik made a decision to construct a ZOO in which would mainly be farm animals and wild native species.

When the first settlers arrived in Iceland, no animal except foxes lived in these parts.

All other types were imported and adapted to the local conditions. Cows were brought from England, France, and Norway; goats arrived with the first inhabitants. Now, centuries later, an Icelandic sheep is in huge demand in the US and Canada, pigeons are bred for aesthetic purposes. The history of each breed can be found in the zoo.

The main inhabitants of the Park include: horses, sheep, goats, foxes, cattle, pigs, minks, deer, seals, hens, turkeys, pigeons, rabbits, guinea pigs, geese, ducks, dogs, and cats. In the park wild birds are constantly being treated. The pleasure of the zoo has grown in this country. Getting acquainted with farm animals you can feel like a farmer: milking cows, shearing sheep, feeding the hens. In recreation places guests can play games, relax, go cycling, horseback riding, etc.

Mansion Hofdi House

The Ministry of Foreign Affairs of Iceland has officially stated, "We cannot confirm or deny the information that in the house lives a ghost." But one of the British diplomats,

John Greenaway, who lived for a long time in a beautiful mansion in Iceland, claimed that he saw the ghost of the young woman every night in the house.

Moreover, the diplomat convinced the authorities to refuse to use the mansion as a dwelling for the consuls. As a consequence, in 1952, the Government of Iceland became the house owner, since it's used for official receptions and meetings of the municipality. Among the most renowned guests of the Hofdi-house mansion have been the King of Norway, Presidents of France and Italy, the Queen of England and Queen of Denmark, Chancellor Willy Brandt of Germany, and many well-known politicians.

But, of course, the most historically important meeting was held at the Hofdi house in 1986, between U.S. President Ronald Reagan and the Soviet Union head Mikhail Gorbachev. This meeting effectively ended the Cold War. In memory of the meeting in the building hang the flags of the USA and the USSR. The old-timers say that the house is built on an ancient burial ground of Vikings.

Viking Maritime Museum

Welcome to the Museum at the seafront. Iceland's history, present, and future are closely connected with seafaring. This activity determines the character of the nation; it is difficult to understand this country without knowing its maritime history. Exhibitions at the Viking Maritime Museum allow you to look at the relationship between Iceland and the sea for centuries; they illustrate the development of the fleet from rowing boats to modern trawlers and powerful cargo ships.

The main highlight of the Museum is "Odinn". It's a legendary ship. It was the best patrol and rescue vessel, towing almost 200 ships in distress to a safe place. The Coast Guard vessel was built in Aalborg in Denmark in 1959. It has a displacement of 910 tons, length 63 m, and a specially reinforced hull for navigation in ice. Its most powerful weapon is the 57 mm gun located on the nose. The Viking Maritime Museum has a fun gift shop. There you can find a lot of interesting items, very bright with an Icelandic twist: Souvenirs, toys, books for children and adults, CDs of Icelandic folk music. The museum is open throughout the year.

Icelandic Phallological Museum

The Icelandic phallus Museum, was founded in 1997 by a former teacher, Sigurdur Hardarson. For 37 years he taught history and Spanish at Reykjavík. His unusual hobby started in childhood after he received a gift of a whip made from a bull penis.

Hardarson started collecting exhibits from around the country. Their sizes range from 2 mm. to 170 cm, for example, the phallus of a blue whale. A phallus of a hamster you only can see through a magnifying glass. Many of the exhibits were supplied by local fishermen. In the slaughterhouse, Hardarsson got the bodies of farm animals. After commercial whaling had been banned, the owner of the museum began his own hunt for the phallus. He took the washed up bodies of large animals to cast.

The penis of a polar bear was received from the hunters who shot the animal, drifting on an ice floe. Big money was paid for the sex organ of an elephant, the length of which is almost a meter. The museum has penises of all mammals that live in Iceland. In addition, the exhibition features many items of phallic art, such as a lampshade made of the scrotum of a bull and an engraving depicting the circumcision of Christ. All around the museum is decorated with carved wooden penises.

All phalluses are stored in formaldehyde or have been dried and are hanging on the walls. A cane was made from a particularly large bull penis. In preparing the collection, Charterstone helped his family, though not without embarrassment. He considers himself a true enthusiast and says you can always find one better than the previous exhibit. Originally the collection was housed in the office of Sigurdur Thorarinsson, but after he retired, he had the idea to put the exhibits on public display. For this purpose, he received a grant from the city council.

A German collector wanted to buy this collection, but Hardarson refused, explaining that it's unique and should be in his home country. The museum has become popular with tourists, most of them women. In addition, the museum argued that the showpieces of the folklore section are nothing like the phalluses of trolls and elves and one-eyed monsters. Sigurdur said that the penis of the elf, which is described in the museum catalog as "big and old," is one of his favorites.

The exhibition includes 55 whale, 36 seal and 118 various mammals' penises, and one penis that belonged to a man. The museum received the long-awaited donor organ in June 2011, but this showpiece was received after traumatic amputation and therefore represents a gray-brown, wrinkled mass in a jar of formaldehyde. Therefore, the proposal of the museum to purchase a "fresh" exhibit is still valid.

Nightlife. Nightclubs and Discos in Reykjavik.

Night "cream" for the young people in Iceland is available in one place—in nightclub Bohem. This venue is a kind of a mix between a bar, a restaurant, and a club, but that's what makes Bohem so popular. Here are lovely girls on the stage, who can stir up the crowd of dancers; meanwhile, bartenders, skillfully manipulating behind the counter, one after the other, serve delicious drinks and cocktails at a reasonable cost that's available to everyone.

Address: Grensasvegur 7, Reykjavik
Phone: 354-517-3530

The elegant, uniquely decorated Begamot Rooms daily greet visitors who want to enjoy the delicacies of Icelandic cuisine. At night this place is transformed and becomes one of the night–clubs in the city. Everyone—famous singers, politicians, tourists and ordinary citizens—who is searching for fun, great music, great show and just perfect service has chosen this club for this.

Address: Vegamotastig 4, Reykjavik
Phone: 354-511-3040

Maybe night-club Nasa will not compare, for example, with the dance floors of Ibiza, but you're unlikely to find a better place in Iceland. Top-rated bands of Iceland perform here like the regular music festivals that attract a huge number of participants not only from Iceland but from other European countries. For example, the jazz festival or the days of hardcore.

Address: Austurvollur square, Reykjavik
Phone: 354-511-1313

Nightclub Astro knows what offer to visitors to return them here again. Fiery rhythms of dance music and sexy "Go-Go" girls—this is only a small part of what awaits visitors. Don't forget about the bar, located at the club, because it invites all to enjoy the best drinks, including cocktails, beer, wines, champagne, and cognacs.

Address: Austurstraeti 22, Reykjavik
Phone: 354-552-9222

There is no hotter place in cool Iceland than night-club Pravda. Popular mainly among students, this club offers its guests the chance to enjoy the romance of the northern night, under the sounds of popular dance tracks and hip-hop. It will help you relax and fully immerse yourself in the atmosphere of entertainment, which in the night-club Pravda is more than enough.

Address: Austurstraeti 22, Reykjavik
Phone: 354-552-9222

Like most nightlife of Iceland, Apotek is a café by day, offering its guests a fun mix of Icelandic and European cuisine with a smoking hot Argentinean grill. But at night it's a different institution, the door of which bursts from just unreal musical rhythms that can lift the mood of anyone. The only thing you need to remember coming here is about clothes: sneakers and jeans at the Apotek are not popular.

Address: Austurstraeti 16 Reykjavik
Phone: 354-575-7900

Q combines a nightclub and a bar. It is very convenient coming here in the afternoon, guests can enjoy great drinks, and at night they can join the noisy crowd dancing on the small dance floor. The local Q Bar is famous as a popular place for gay people, but that doesn't mean that the venue is only for people with different sexual orientations. On the contrary, Q will welcome any visitor!

Address: Ingolfsstraeti 3, Reykjavik
Phone: 354-578-7868

Cafe, bistro, restaurant, bar and night-club all in one charming place; Solon, offers entertainment and recreation for every taste. At night the small dance floor club welcomes all its guests with relaxed rhythms of modern compositions while the bar located on the ground floor simply cannot accommodate visitors who prefer a quiet conversation over a cocktail, wine or beer; instead, there's loud music.

Address: Bankastraeti 7a, Reykjavik
Phone: 354-562-3232

Night-club Gaukur A Stong, after its opening in 1983, started to work as a pub. During the enforcement of the ban on beer, it offered its guests a signature cocktail, bjorliki, consisting of vodka and non-alcoholic beer. Later, the pub was rebuilt, turning it into a hot night-club, where new Icelandic performers play on weekdays, but on weekends the audience warms up popular DJs and famous music groups.

Address: Tryggvagata 22, Reykjavik

Phone: 354-551-1556

Shopping in Reykjavik

Iceland is considered to be one of the most expensive countries in Europe, but now the difference with other major cities no longer seems so shocking. The food here is expensive. You need to know where to shop, to save and pleasure yourself and others in Reykjavik

One of the cheapest food networks in Iceland is considered to be the "Bonus" market's. You can easily recognize them by the logo of a pink piggy-bank on a yellow background. In Reykjavik,store "Bonus" is on the main street Laugavegur. The prices are not high in the stores "Kronan" and "Kolaportid market" near the bus stop in Lækjartorg. At the market, you can stock up on everything you need on Saturdays and Sundays until about three in the afternoon.

Most of the shops in Iceland are open from Monday to Thursday. Work hours: from 9 to 18, to Friday 9-19, Saturday 10 to 16 hours. Also some of them are open on Sundays; supermarkets open until 8 p.m. Most of the shops accept card payments, but some offer discounts only for cash. If you are a tourist and shop in Iceland, you have the possibility to return the VAT for the purchased goods, if their total value is above 4000 ISK (Icelandic kroner) for purchases in one shop.

In the store, you have to pay the sum in full and warn the seller that you need a refund of VAT. The seller will give you a special filled-out form with a receipt for the purchase. A VAT refund will be provided at the airport in the window "Tax refund." Then you're supposed to show the goods to customs and ask them to put a stamp on the form. In most stores, you can get a brochure called "Shopping in Iceland," which shows the current VAT rates and the possibility of return.

Here is a rough rate.
Exchange rate $1 approximately 100–120 ISK
Food
Bread, $1.5–2.5 about 150–250 ISK;

Oil, $1.5 about 150 ISK;

Eggs (10 pieces) $4–5 about 400-600 ISK;

Milk will cost you $1.5 about 150 ISK;

A cake in the café $2.5–5 about 250-500 ISK;

A glass of wine or beer $5–7 about 600 – 800 ISK;

Pizza pizzeria $15 about 1500 ISK.

Fuel at gas stations will cost $2 about 175-190 ISK and the price of gasoline often change.

Liquid dishwashing costs $7 about 700 ISK;

Soap dispenser $2.5 about 250 ISK.

What to Buy as a Gift in Iceland

Pay attention to the wool products from Icelandic sheep; it's perfect quality, soft wool. A feature of this wool is that it repels water and is very warm; sweaters, hats and gloves are manufactured from this wool. In our days, mainly things made of wool are produced by machines, but if you try, you can find hand-knitted items. The cost of woolen sweaters starts from $80 about 8000 ISK. Products made of sheep wool are very expensive, but they are great in quality. Hats or gloves are approximately $30–50 about 3000–5000 ISK.

There are many small shops that sell crafts and handmade goods, porcelain figurines, paintings, glass and jewelry in Reykjavík. Of course, a great gift with a local flavor will be Icelandic folk music, you can buy a lot of CDs with ethnic-rock and record world-known Icelandic singers: Björk, Sigur Rós, and others.

Designer fashion in Reykjavik presents several interesting boutiques that are worth attention too. For example, sisters Einvera fashion designers designed clothes under the brand "Kalda". This is a simple and modern style. Address: Laugarvegur 35, 101 reykjavík). Kiosk is a trendy boutique, which is jointly owned by, 9 designers. Moreover, they work in turns. They offer an interesting range of flowers and materials. Here you'll find a collection of accessories and jewelry.

Like all of Iceland, fashion here is extremely different from any other countries primarily for its unpredictability and the presence of ethnic motifs and avant-garde processing. The cost of products starts from 100–200 euros.

In Iceland you can buy special cheese and dried fish; however, those delicacies are not for everyone. Immerse yourself in a world of the harsh and peculiar Icelandic worldview.

Discount card of Reykjavik:

Upon arriving in Reykjavik do not forget about the possibility of acquiring a <u>Reykjavik Welcome Card</u>*. With it, you can save your money in many places in the city. For more details, you can read the information on this card* <u>here</u>*.* <u>*http://www.visitreykjavik.is/travel/reykjavik-city-card*</u>

CHAPTER 6 Tours in Iceland

The West Coast of Iceland is mainly made up of fjords, forests, and mountains. It looks much like Norway. There is the highest waterfall of the Island—Glymur (650 feet or 198 m). Snaefellbaer is a territory located in the southwest of the island Snaefellsnes. Most of it is inhabited, and on the west there is a national park "under the ice cap". This ice cap is considered to be the biggest one in Iceland, highly raised over Peninsula; it is known as one of seven energy centers of the Earth.12km of ridge rocks, Látrabjarg, stretch along the coast. Their height varies from 40 to 400 m. There is the westernmost point of Iceland and Europe—Lighthouse Bjargtangi.

Blooming Lupine flowers on the Stokksnes headland. South Eastern Icelandic coast.

This place is perfect for bird watching, among which you can see the symbol of the country—the sea parrot (puffin).

You should see the ice caps in southern Iceland, ice lagoon, southern waterfalls and beaches with black volcanic sand. All this beauty is located in southern Iceland. Every day you can take a tour to travel there from Reykjavik, you can have an excursion. If you travel by car, book a hotel in Vik for several days. Staying there, you'll be able to visit all places within 2–3 days. Vik is the southernmost city of the island. The major sightseeing in Vik consists of a secluded, picturesque, white church with a red roof and cliffs, Reynisdrangar, raising 215feet or 66m above sea level. According to Icelandic legend, in the Reynisdrangar cliffs are trolls hardened in the early dawn.

View of Reynisdrangar rock formations on Reynisfjara Beach at sunrise, near Vic, Iceland.

Most of the southern coast consists of sand, a large number of ice rivers flow into the sea here.

Vestmannaeyjar consists of fifteen islands in the southern Iceland coast. They have been formed by volcanic explosions for the last 10 thousand years.

I reckon the perfect duration of stay in Iceland is ten days. You can visit all the exciting places and take your sweet time. If you would like to spend several days at some places you like, you'd better go for two weeks.

It is best to travel round the island. This way you will see almost all the exciting places. If you are limited in time, you can put up in the central area and see the south of the island where the most exciting and fascinating places are concentrated.

Must-visit places are the Blue Lagoon, Ice Lagoon, and Geysers.

The Golden Ring is a—popular tour itinerary in southern Iceland; it starts from Reykjavik, goes across central Iceland (where the major part of the sightseeing is located) and goes back to Reykjavik. Approximate duration - about 8 hours.

Three main stops during the Golden Ring tour are Thingvellir, Waterfall Gullfoss and Geyser Valley Haukadalur. Thingvellir is a national park, registered as a UNESCO World Heritage Center in 2004. In the year 930, the first parliament of Iceland was founded here–the eldest parliament in the world. Gullfoss, word-for-word translation- Golden Waterfall, is considered to the most beautiful waterfall of the country. There is well-known Geysir in Geyser Valley, Haukadalur, from which were named all other hot springs on the planet. Currently, Geysir has lost its power and breaks out to the surface rarely. There is a far more active geyser in the same area Strokkur—tossing out vapor and a water column at the height of 60–100 feet or 20–30 meters each 5-10 minutes.

Also, in the "Golden Ring" tour, there is a stop near a solidified volcanic vent, volcano Kerid www.kerid.is. At the bottom of the vent a lake has formed along with a village, Hveragerdi, where exotic fruits and vegetables are grown in green-houses thanks to the thermal springs, church Skálholt and geothermal power station, Nesjavellir.

Kerid is a crater lake in Iceland. The lake is located in the western volcanic zone of the country. Lake Kerid, like other volcanoes in this area, consists primarily of red volcanic rock. The crater width is about 550 feet, and its diameter is 1,000 feet, its depth 180 feet.

It is approximately 3000 years old. Kerid is among the most recognizable volcanic craters. The lake is quite shallow (20 to 45 feet, depending on rainfall and other factors), Because of minerals that enter the water from the soil, the water is opaque and strikingly vivid and is an amazing aquamarine color.

If you move a little bit away from the volcano along the path you can see another amazing sight: the beauty of the earth under your feet will exceed all your expectations. The land is painted in black, red, pink and yellow due to minerals.

In Iceland, there are several similar crater lakes, for example, a geothermal lake, Viti. This is geothermal and very mineral-rich water. This area was used during testing of the Apollo program to prepare astronauts for landing on the moon.

Tour to Whalefjord and Videy Island.

Make sure you take a tour or drive to the beautiful fjord called Hvalfjordur, which means Whalefjord, located north of Reykjavik.

Whalefjord's length is about 18.5 miles, width 3 miles and depth is up to 280 feet. The name of the fjord is self-explanatory. From way back, whales came into the fjord and till now there is the Iceland's only functional dock for ocean giants charting.

The road will lead you through a 3.5miles long subaqueous tunnel, torn through solid rock. There are many beautiful places where you can stop to have a walk and take photos. You'll see freewheeling lands and pastures with animals, numerous rivulets and waterfalls streaming down the cliffs, framing the fjord. You'll visit the uninhabited world of silence and voicelessness, the world of nothing but the sky, the sea, and the wind.

The road along the fjord coast will lead you to the church, Hallgrímskirkja Saurbæ. In the XVIIth century, the most well-known   Icelandic ecclesiastical   poet Hallgrimur Petursson (1614 - 1674) was a senior priest of it. The church stands in solitude, on the shore of Whale Fjord. Beauty and the vastness of surrounding landscape are breathtaking!

There is a picturesque intermount valley. You can enjoy the view of the magnificent mountains and rapid mountain rivers with clear water peopled with salmon.

Several small islands, one of which is called Videy, are located opposite Reykjavik, in the sea gulf.

They are truly picturesque, covered with dense green grass and having an unusual coastline.

Many species of birds are nesting and brooding on the islands.There, regardless of the close location of the big city, birds feel perfectly safe. The same can be said for everywhere in Iceland though.

Tours to Videy Island are available for tourists of any age and will bring much joy to you. On a cute, small vessel, you will sail to the island and will have an unhurried walk along its wild paths. You'll see the archeological site of an ancient monastery and church of unusual architecture built at the end of the XVIIIth century.

You'll see the Holy Mary statue standing on the hill alone. You'll find Peace Tower particularly interesting—a unique piece of modern art. The designer was Yoko Ono, wife of legendary John Lennon. An intense ray of light, visible tens of kilometers around, rushes up the high dark sky from the deep well. It is an amazing sight!

A beautiful view of Reykjavik and the opposite site of the Gulf can be seen from the Iceland.

Vestmannaeyjar is an archipelago made of several volcanic islands lying off the South Coast of Iceland. The only inhabited island of the archipelago is called Heimaey. A city with the same name is located on it. Vestmannaeyja City, with a population of 4,5 thousand people, is one the largest fishing ports in the country.

Vestmannaeyjar is called the "tourist pearl" of Iceland. It stands back from major itineraries but inevitably draws the admiration of tourists.

The pristine nature of the islands, surrounding landscapes, people's way of life and a century's history of this country are unique.

Vestmannaeyjar is a photographer's paradise. You can watch cute sea parrots (puffins) from several meters distance, and you can see whales from the shore if you are lucky enough.

You can walk on the fields of solidified lava, along with the Nothern Pompeii Street; climb the summit of sleeping volcano Eldfell, feeling its warm breath under your feet and watch well-known volcano Eyjafjallajokull at short range.

Exhibits of the local historical museum and collection of sea animals, birds and minerals are quite interesting. The unique functional church, Staffkirkja, (the only copy of an Old Norse church in Iceland) can't leave anybody unmoved.

You'll feel that special, steady and easy pace of life of this genuine upcountry part of Iceland surrounded by silence and the pristine, unspoiled nature of the North Atlantic.

A tour around the South Coast will bring you lots of unforgettable impressions. The vast territories of South Iceland delight the eye of the traveler with its natural landscapes: wide meadows with emerald-green grass and peacefully feeding sheep and horses, mountain groups of the most bizarre shapes, black beaches many kilometers long, ice caps shining in the sun, and stunning waterfalls.

On your way, make sure to use the submarine tunnel built under the Whale Fjord.

Tingvallavatn

Tingvallavatn is the largest lake in Iceland; it is located in the southeast of this state.

It has an area of 84sq.km (32.5 square-miles); moreover, it is 114 m (374 ft.) deep.

Interestingly, the lake bed is 13m (43 ft.) below sea level. Lake on Ting fields is how the translation of Tingvallavatn sounds.

The world-renowned fissure Silfra is located in Tingvallavatn and extends along the bottom of the lake.

The average water temperature here fluctuates from +1 to +5 degrees, so all dives are made in dry suits. The lake never freezes because of strong undercurrents. A lot of grottoes and caves, as well as a very beautiful gorge, Silfra, attract many divers from around the world. The gorge can be divided into three parts. The first one is the "Chess cabinet". There are 40 meter (131 ft.) high boulders at the bottom, resembling chess pieces. The second one is 300m wide and called the "Silfra Cathedral". The third one is "Silfra Lagoon," it is not deep, and so the sunshine beats its way to the very bottom. The light glistening on algae creates exciting and amazing images.

https://www.extremeiceland.is/en/activity-tours-iceland/diving-iceland

Volcano Laki or Lakagigar

The Laki volcano is located in southern Iceland, which is a massive volcanic fissure and lava field with lots of craters. The volcano is sometimes called the Craters of Laki.

Laki is located within the Natural Park of Skaftafell.

The Craters of Laki stretch for a distance of 15 miles; it's possible to count more than 110 lava cones. The height of some of the craters reaches 2500 feet, but on average they tower over the basalt surface to a height of about 300 feet. During the years 1783-1784 in Iceland occurred one of the most catastrophic eruptions in history. Volcano Laki, along with the nearby volcanoes, erupted for eight months. The power of the eruption was estimated at six points on the Volcanic Explosivity Index. Lava flows coming from 50 feet per crack, for eight months covered a distance of over 100 miles. In the air were ejected enormous clouds of ash and toxic sulfur compounds. This natural disaster killed half of all livestock in the country and about 25% of its population.

Volcanic ash was contained in the atmosphere over half of Eurasia, and this caused a temperature drop in the Northern Hemisphere. This eruption led to crop failures in Europe in 1784, to drought in India and Japan, to a long and cold winter in North America, and grave consequences in North Africa. According to experts, the consequences of this deadly eruption on a global scale led to the deaths of more than six million people.

You Can Travel to Iceland by Yourself

In a rental car http://www.rentalcars.com/en/country/is/ or use the services of local guides. http://www.icelandguide.is

Learn the main routes in this chapter, and it will be easier to plan the optimal route for you.

You can simply follow one of the routes as described below.

Multi-day itineraries around the island, the routes on the west and east fjords, the inland routes, the single-day routes, routes to the lakes, waterfalls, and coasts of Iceland.

The route is planned, where and when you can watch the whales and millions of nesting birds that are not afraid of tourists, and where better to swim to the icebergs and where you need to hunt for the Northern Lights.

Follow the route description, and it will be easy for you to focus on each aspect of travel.

The Photo Tour around the Island and a Trip on Yachts along the Western Fjords.

If you want to plan your vacation yourself, in this chapter you will find a description of one of the possible routes. I would recommend paying attention to the information in this chapter. This information will be especially useful for your trip. Also, this chapter will be of interest to all readers. The route is exciting, and you will learn the facts about many interesting places in Iceland. This expedition was held in Iceland with my participation in 2017.

Country: Iceland.

Kind of vacation: car trip with campers, adventure, trekking, yachting.

Necessary requirements: normal physical preparation.

Duration: 10–16 days

You may need money for: camper rental, parking and overnight stays, fuel for the whole travel segment in campers, transfers to and from the airport, minibus rentals for transferring your team from yachts to camper cars and back, services of drivers, entrance fees to national parks along the route, accommodation at the hotel in Reykjavik, accommodation on a yacht in cabins, rental of a comfortable yacht, skipper services, parking in marinas, fuel, cleaning of the yacht, bed linen, kayaks, rental of necessary equipment, local Icelandic guide services.

Also plan the costs for your flight to Iceland and back, meals, optional events of your choice, and personal insurance.

Route: Keflavik-Reykjavik Airport, Hvammstangi, Glaumbær, Akureyri, Myvatn, Godafoss, Námaskarð, Jarðböðin, Husavik, Ásbyrgi, Dettifoss, Egilsstadir, Hengifoss, Litlanesfoss, Reyðarfjörður, Djupиvogur, Hofn, Jokulsarlon, Skaftafell, Vatnajökull, Svartifoss, Vik, Reynisfjara, Dyrhólaey, Skógarfoss, Seljalandsfoss, Selfoss, Reykjadalur, Stóri Geysir, Strokkur, Gullfoss, Þingvallavatn, Thingvellir, Vestfirðir, Ísafjörður, Arnarstapi, Flatey, Reykjavik.

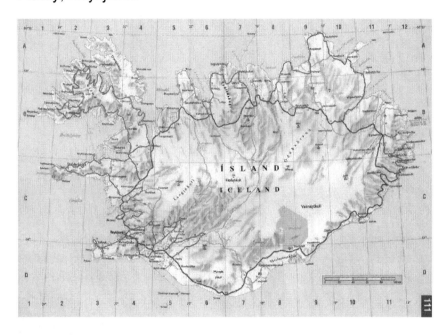

Expedition Program

In brief about the expedition. IMPORTANT:

The route is roughly divided into days. The beginning and end of the day can vary depending on the time spent at each of the stops. In addition, a light day in summer and winter is different and you should consider this too.

The maximum of this route you will explore in the summer.

This route begins in Reykjavik. Upon arrival, you need to stay in a hotel in the city. You can choose and book a hotel here www.galahotels.com or here www.booking.com for example. The day after arrival I recommend that you get acquainted with the local guide to discuss the route. Then you need to decide if you will take the guide with you and after that start the journey. Here are the contacts of some local guides in Reykjavik: Local Guides in Reykjavik Iceland www.toursbylocals.com

This route can be divided into two parts, a land adventure, and a sea route. During the first 8 days of the trip, you can go around the island and see many unique places. Then you will have a choice. You can fly home from Reykjavik or continue your journey. If you continue, then, on the 9th day of the expedition, you can go to Isafjordur and take a yacht there. After that you will find amazing sailing along the western fjords for several days.

So, let's go, friends!

Day one - (arrival day) - Arrival at Keflavik Airport (usually arriving after 4 pm, but most flights arrive around 23:00 local time). You can agree with the guide about the meeting at the airport in advance. I recommend that you immediately buy a local SIM card to have the Internet en route.

Go to your hotel in Reykjavik (30 miles) for the night.

Dine in the hotel or, if you have the time and desire, walk around the city. But it's better to save your strength for the next day.

Day two - (day trip 255 miles/410 km) - Wake up early, have breakfast, gather. Leave rooms in the hotel and go to the city to get a camper. Instruction of drivers. Acceptance and transfer of equipment.

Stop by the supermarket. Buy necessary food, drinks, etc. for a comfortable trip.

On this day of travel, the biggest crossing of the route is to be made. So do not waste time and try to get ready as soon as possible. Go towards Borgarfjordur, an interesting area with a rich cultural and historical heritage. Further, the route runs to the north of Iceland through the region of Skagafjord, which is known for the breeding of horses.

On the way, stop, and you can take a lot of photos and meet the local horses. All around you will find wonderful nature.

In the afternoon you should get to the small fishing town of Hvammstangi. Not far from the town, a lot of fur seals sail in the sun. You can try to take many beautiful pictures with these lovely inhabitants of the northern seas. Do not spend a lot of time in Hvammstangi and continue your trip in the camper. Along the way, you can stop for lunch, drink coffee and stretch your legs a little.

Also try to visit the museum in the village of Glaumbær. Here is a beautifully restored ancient building. You can see how the Icelanders lived before, their ancient way of life and foundations.

Then drive to Akureyri, the main city in the north of Iceland. In this northern town, you can spend the night or two nights, depending on how much time you have. It will be easy for you to find a suitable nice place for parking your camper. In such places, there is water nearby and electricity as a rule. Or you can just stop at any place you like. After all, if you travel by camper, you are the most mobile and not dependent on anyone. The sun sets very late in the summer, around 10 pm. If you arrive earlier, you will have time to get grills, tables and camping chairs set up in the light of day. You can cook food and eat directly in nature and rest after that.

Day three - (day trip 155 miles/250km) - Try not to sleep for a long time in the morning. Wake up. Wash your face. Cook breakfast. Pick up any stuff and trash scattered around the cars. Move forward; this day you have a route rich in the impression of Iceland.

Dedicate a whole day to the wonders of the nature reserve of Lake Myvatn. This place is known as one of the most beautiful natural regions of Iceland.

Myvatn, as a nature reserve, was organized in 1968 and has an area of more than 115 square miles. In the reserve, there are natural complexes of volcanic plateau and Lake Myvatn. This is not the simplest lake, and it is the center of geothermal and volcanic activity. Lava fields and volcanic craters so brightly reflect everything that happens in the bowels of the earth.

The lake is not very deep, its depth reaches somewhere around 15 feet, and the area it occupies is 14 square miles. The lake divided into two different parts. On the surface of the lake there are about fifty islands. The minimum amount of precipitation falls in the area of Lake Myvatn throughout the year. So it is considered the driest area in Iceland. This feature is associated with the glacier Vatnajokull, the big glacier located nearby to Myvatn, and protects this area from precipitation.

Thanks to the volcanic heat, the most beautiful pond water in the country does not freeze all year round. As a result of which many waterfowl nest on it, especially ducks. Ducks live here more than anywhere else in Europe—more than 20 thousand individuals of 16 different species including the mallard duck, teal duck, crouch duck, black duck, gogol duck, swine, pintail, and other species of ducks. Clouds of steam shooting from the ground, gurgling mud puddles, lava poles and streams and other signs of volcanic activity enhance the uniqueness of these lakeside landscapes and attract many tourists to the park.

On the way to Myvatn, stop by the very impressive Waterfall Godafoss, this name translates as "The Waterfall of the Gods". Next, visit the labyrinths of the lava Dimmuborgir, a huge area where you will find a walk through an impressive volcanic "city of lava". Locals believe that elf people secretly live there.

Another of the main attractions of Myvatn is Námaskarð, a geothermal area where you will walk, and right under your feet will come out a sizzling steam from the ground. Do not miss the Krafla area and the volcanic crater Viti.

In the afternoon, snack and head to Jarðböðin. This is an analog of the well-known and untwisted "Blue Lagoon", but tourists are few in comparison to other sights. Spend some time with pleasure in the open-air geothermal springs located to the east of Lake Myvatn.

In the evening, return to Akureyri for the second night. Prepare dinner yourself or go to a local cafe and go for a rest after dinner.

Day four - (day trip 210 miles/340km) - Back to the road.

Today, you are waiting for fascinating adventures. In summer, the day in Iceland is very long and you can expect to see everything in the sunlight. First stop by in the charming village of Husavik.

Husavik is a small Icelandic village in the northeast of the country on the shores of the Arctic Ocean, located near Akureyri. The name of the village is translated as "the bay where the house stands". One of the oldest settlements in Iceland here arose accidentally when several members of the Garðar Svavarsson expedition were forced to winter on the coast.

Of course, the primary business for the inhabitants of Husavik is fishing. In local restaurants on the waterfront, you can taste delicious dishes made with freshly caught fish. The menu of the restaurant changes almost daily depending on the catch. You can have breakfast in Husavik and then explore the village and visit museums.

Husavik offers tourists the opportunity to take exciting and unusual excursions. The village often acts as a starting point for travel to the north of Iceland. One of the most popular trips is going on a ship to the open sea to observe whales, which are especially numerous in this area of Iceland. Husavik is called the capital of whale watching. If you do not plan to sail on the yachts at the end of the trip, here is the best place to go out to sea for whale watching. The cost of the tour is around $120.

In Husavik there are two interesting museums, one of them dedicated to whales and the second—to phalluses. In the two-story building of the Whale Museum, there are many photos of these animals as well as skeletons of whales. The phallus museum is an exposition of the conserved sexual organs of various animals of the globe. Only the human phallus you will not see here. For the time being.

After lunch, slide towards the Ásbyrgi Canyon. According to one of the legends, the canyon got its shape when Sleipnir, Odin's horse, stepped here with one of his eight hooves and formed a gorge in the shape of a horseshoe with its impressive stone walls of 330 feet high. Here you can trek in the national park. It's a wonderful place. Take a lot of photos.

Then drive south from Ásbyrgi, the road leads you to the mighty Waterfall Dettifoss. This is the largest waterfall in Europe regarding the amount of falling water. It is also called the king of all waterfalls in Iceland! Height is 150 feet, width is 110 yards. The average amount of water passing here reaches 130 thousand gallons per second. It's hard to get here, but the traveler who decides on a long journey to the shores of the Greenland Sea, in which, in the summer, sometimes icebergs swim, will indeed be rewarded for his perseverance. Further, you will pass through the lunar landscape of the mountainous region Mördrudur, where the eastern capital Egilsstadir is located. At sunset here, you can take a lot of photos and video masterpieces. In the evening, find a nice and quiet place to stay overnight. Prepare dinner and rest, spend the night in the Egilsstadir area.

Day five - (day trip 170 miles/270km) - In the morning, waking up rested, first make a small move about 20 miles to the southwest. Then put on your mountain boots and head for a short but beautiful trek to the third highest waterfall in Iceland—the Hengifoss 400-feet waterfall.

Now get ready! The Hengifoss is situated on the river Hengyfossau in the municipality of Skorradalshreppur in Austurland and it flows into the canyon of Fljótsdalsvegur. The path to the waterfall is very beautiful. The gorge forms an amphitheater of basalt columns, along which passes another 100-foot waterfall, Litlanesfoss, which you can also see. Litlanesfoss is famous for its basalt columns of volcanic origin. Similar columns you will see in the area of the town Vik on the "Black Beach", Reynisfjara. The name Litlanesfoss means "waterfall - younger brother" and it was so named because of its proximity to the "steeper" fall, Hengifoss.

Hengifoss - the third highest waterfall in Iceland or maybe the second. The Internet and official statistics say that the height of the waterfall is 128 meters (420 feet), and on the sign nearby it altitudes of 188 meters (615 feet) are indicated. Hengifoss is surrounded by basaltic rocks, between which are thin layers of red clay. This is the uniqueness of the waterfall and its main feature. If you're lucky enough to see a rainbow in this place, it's something incredibly beautiful.

After walking, return to your campers and drive on. Now it's time to explore the eastern fjords. Start with the Reydarfjordur fjord. In a small town of the same name you can visit a museum, a private collection that includes most Icelandic minerals.

Take the fjords slowly. They are wonderful places. Stop often to photograph local beauty. For lunch, you can stop into Djupivogur, a small, cute town with stone statues in the form of eggs of every Icelandic bird. It looks funny.

Continue to drive along the fjords in the direction of Southeast Iceland. The road winds through the mountains with crazy, beautiful views all around. Drive through the Almannaskarð Tunnel, and in the evening you will arrive in a small town, Hofn, where you can stay. Pick a beautiful place to stay overnight. Put up your camp and cook dinner. Share your impressions, put photos on Facebook if the internet allows.

Day six - (day trip 170 miles/280 km) - Wake up early! You need to see many places today. Do not forget to have a good breakfast. Turn on your cars and move from night parking to the glacial lagoon "Jokulsarlon". This amazing lagoon appeared just a few decades ago as a result of the Vatnajökull glacier breakaway. Now the ice lagoon is increasing in size rapidly. In the lagoon, you can walk around and enjoy spectacular views of icebergs, mountains, and glaciers or you can float in the lagoon between the icebergs on a speedboat. I recommend!

The cost of an hour's walk on the boat: approximately $100–$120 per person.

In this place were filmed some Hollywood blockbusters, *Lara Croft: Tomb Raider* and *James Bond: Die Another Day*.

Producer Stuart Kornfeld said about the shootings in this place: "Iceland is an amazing country, where the quality of light differs from any location on Earth. It's like switching from a 35-millimeter world to a 70-millimeter one".

After visiting the lagoon, walk a little on the sea coast among the thousands of pieces of ice that are thrown out by the sea to the black sands.

It looks unusual and wonderful.

After a short trip (18 miles) you will get to another glacial lagoon. It is a beautiful place with an incredible view of the descending glacier.

Then, drive along the route to the Skaftafell National Park. This national park is located next to the largest glacier in Europe, Vatnajökull, with an ice thickness of up to 2000 feet.

The glacier occupies 12% of the area of Iceland. In Skaftafell you will find a huge number of trekking routes of different levels of complexity.

First, leave your camping cars in the parking lot, and go to the track to one gorgeous waterfall—Svartifoss. The descending basalt columns from which the waterfall flows have been compared to a church organ. The round trip takes about 1 to 1.5 hours and runs through an equipped and uncomplicated trail.

Returning to the parking lot, you can eat a pretty tasty lunch at a local restaurant and then go on another trek to the foot of the glacier. It takes about one hour. After all these exciting walks, drive towards the town of Vik.

Along the way, admire the magnificent Martian landscapes of the Mýrdalssandur lava fields that are covered with moss.

In the evening, get to Vik, and try to arrive at the Black Beach at sunset. Then stop your cars in any place you like. In local shops, you can replenish food, water, and alcohol. Finish your current adventure and get ready for bed.

Day seven - (day trip 80 miles/130km). Although today you have small crossings for miles, the number of cult places are very high. Have breakfast and start your journey early. If yesterday you did not get to the basalt columns of Reynisfjara, then first stop by them. Take a walk and admire the scenery, it's very beautiful. There you can drink your morning coffee in a local cafe.

Then go to the Dyrhólaia Rock. There is a lighthouse there, and an impressive view of the ocean and a giant arch opens. If you're lucky, you'll see a large number of the famous northern puffin bird there.

After that, get down the Dyrhólaey and drive about 30 minutes to another unusual object, the old American airplane stuck on the seashore. The United States Navy Douglas Super DC-3 airplane experienced some severe icing and made an emergency landing in this places in the year 1973. Luckily, no one was hurt. The plane now is an attractive place for all kinds of unusual photos brought from Iceland. The walk is about a 1.5 to 2-hour round trip. Around the plane, there are many more beautiful species, and there the fantasy of the photographer has a lot of material to look at.

After plenty of photographs, drive around an hour to one of the most beautiful waterfalls in Iceland, the Skógarfoss waterfall. If there is sun, then Skógarfoss will be all in rainbows and it's incredibly beautiful. Those interested can climb along the path to the top of the waterfall, which is wonderful. At the foot of the waterfall, dine at one of the two local restaurants.

Drive 18 miles along the main road towards Reykjavik and you will get to another very famous Icelandic waterfall, Seljalandsfoss. Under this waterfall you can walk and watch the incredibly beautiful spectacle of the falling water, which is refracted in the rays of the evening sun. It's really a fantastic sight. Wait for the evening light and you can get a lot of good photos.

Take a walk around all three Seljalandfoss waterfalls and then head to the town of Selfoss, where you can spend the night. It's about 40 miles from the Seljalandsfoss waterfall. There are many restaurants and cafes. There is a supermarket in which you can replenish supplies of provisions.

Day eight - (day trip 100 miles/170km). Start your morning with delightful entertainment. Take a small trip (about 10 miles) in the direction of Hveragerði to Reykjadalur Hot Spring Thermal River. There you will have a walk along the equipped trail about four miles in the valley of the geysers with the natural hot river, Reykjadalur. There, swim and rest, and enjoy an incredible atmosphere. After that, go back to the cars; you can drink coffee or tea at a local cafe, and then go to the so-called "Golden Ring" of Iceland. This route goes through several very spectacular and favorite places in Iceland, which every tourist and traveler is obligated to see. Therefore, there are always many lively people here.

Start with one of the first famous sights of Iceland, the valley of the Haukadalur geysers. Here the Great Geysir is sleeping. This Geysir is the father of geysers and erupts irregularly, and over the last century, due to earthquakes, its activity changed several times. "Father Geyser" can sleep for years, but sometimes it is specially woken up on Independence Day (June 17) with soapy water. The fountain, which it throws into the air, reaches 200 feet. At fifty yards, the Strokkur Geyser spouts water 30 meters (100 feet) into the air every 5--7 minutes. You can watch this geyser with other tourists. The main thing is to choose the right side for observations so that during the ejection you do not get wet from head to toe!

After the Valley of the Geysers, visit the majestic Gullfoss Waterfall or "Golden Waterfall". If you are lucky with the weather, you can watch two rainbows just above the waterfall. The Gullfoss Waterfall is on the glacial river Hvítá, which, in Icelandic, means the White River. This river is one of the longest rivers in Iceland. It is born from thawed water flowing down from the huge Langjökull Glacier, the second largest glacier in Iceland. In this place the river Hvítá is shallow, but with a rapid current. The color of the water varies and can be milky white, cloudy gray, or greenish. It all depends on the composition of the layer of melting ice. Going on a trip to Gullfoss, you never know what color the water will be. It's always a surprise. There are two free parking areas near the waterfall, upper and lower, connected by a pedestrian ladder. On the upper parking is a one-story building, inside there is a cafe with a good choice of food and bakery, a large gift shop and the usual facilities. Here you can have lunch.

Next, go to Lake Thingvallavatn. This is the largest lake in Iceland with volcanic islands. Near to the lake is situated the Thingvellir National Park. This a historic place for Icelanders and the national flag is proudly developing here. Here, in the year 930, the first meeting of the All-Icelandic Parliament took place. In the year 1000, Christianity was accepted as a single religion in this place. Thingvellir also played a role in modern history—in this place, in 1944, independent Iceland was proclaimed. Besides its historical significance, Thingvellir also has incredible natural beauty landscapes, formed by the Peningagia Canyon. Thingvellir is also considered one of the geological wonders of the world, where you can see the effect of movement of tectonic plates. This is the place where North America is separated from Europe.

Day nine - (day trip 18 miles/30km). You need to get to Reykjavik, try to be there by 10 am and return the camper. Now you can continue your journey on yachts. For this you need to take a transfer to the northwest of the island in Ísafjörður, which is on the Vestfirðir Peninsula. On the coast of the Vestfirðir Peninsula are the famous Icelandic fjords. This region occupies 30 percent of the coastline of the whole of Iceland. It is washed by the Atlantic Ocean from the west and southwest sides, and from the northeast side by the Greenland Sea. The area is 3500 square miles. The center is Ísafjörður, there, you can get into yachts. It is better to rent yachts in advance. From Reykjavik it's about 5–6 hours to get to the marina of the city Ísafjörður (about 270 miles). After arrival, you will be settled on boats. You need to get acquainted with the captain and receive all the necessary safety instructions. After that, cook dinner on board and rest.

In the rest days of your vacation, spend a yacht trip in one of the most remote and beautiful regions of Iceland. There are very few tourists. These places are wild and incredibly beautiful. On the way, you will meet dolphins, whales, and killer whales. You will fish and sail in remote villages on the lost islands. See incredible nature and stunning sea sunsets, visit lava caves, go to glaciers, swim in hot springs and much more. This part of the journey you will remember for life for the right reasons!

Most of Iceland is famous for its unprecedented volcanism and the north-western part of the country is the kingdom of the fjords. The capital of all the western fjords could be considered Isafjordur—the largest city in this area of Iceland. The region is extremely sparsely populated. In Isafjordur live more than half the inhabitants of the Vestfirðir region (4000 people). Isafjordur is the capital of the western fjords, but at the same time, it is quite a small fishing town. The history of the city begins back in the year 920 when the first settlers began to appear in its territory. The city was slowly developing; a little later, Norwegian and Icelandic traders settled here. In the sixteenth century, British and German colonies appeared on the territory of Isafjordur. After the Danish administration was established in the city, buildings began to be erected here, which have survived to this day. This is a very picturesque city, located in a beautiful, quiet place. It is surrounded by the calm waters of the fjords and majestic cliffs. Visiting the center, guests of the city can see ancient buildings and wooden panel houses, some of which have not changed at all since the eighteenth century. At that time, the city was one of the largest shelters for whalers and various ships. Here you can visit many interesting local attractions, cafes, bars and restaurants.

At the end of the trip, your yachts will return to Reykjavik, to the marina in the city center. You can have dinner in one of the many central restaurants in the city. On the last day of the trip, in the morning, you can wander around the city on your own and buy souvenirs. Eviction from yachts is usually after lunch. Say goodbye to your captain and Iceland as now is the time to leave.

Tour around the Island

Upon arrival in Iceland, you can stay in Reykjavik.

You can choose your preferred accommodation option in Chapter 3 *WHERE TO STAY WHILE TRAVELING IN ICELAND*

Information about sights, shops and rest in Reykjavik you will find in Chapter 5 *CAPITAL REYKJAVIK*

Day one.

From Reykjavik to Vik (115 miles in transit).

See Eyjafjallajokull Volcano, visit Seljalandsfoss and Skogafoss Waterfalls.

Drive from Reykjavik to the southeast on Road no.1 heading to Vik. After driving 70 miles from the capital, stop off at Seljalandsfoss Waterfall. Let's continue 18 miles to the south and stop at the Skogafoss Waterfall. Until then Vik will remain 20 miles away.

Before Vik, you will meet the famous, after its eruption in 2010, volcano Eyjafjallajokull.

In Vik, you will be able to eat in a local cafe or restaurant. If you are not traveling in a hurry, we recommend you stay the night in Vik.

Until evening you will be able to enjoy nature and beautiful scenery, riding along the southern coast of Iceland.

Day two.

From Vik to Hofn with a stop in Skaftafell National Park and Ice Lagoon (150 miles in transit).

Leaving Vik go east along Road no. 1 to the town of Hof. Here visit Skaftafell (Vatnajokull) desert with geysers and volcanoes in Skaftafell (Vatnajokull) National Park.

20 miles drive east of the Hof is located a beautiful ice lagoon, Jokulsarlon. Turn left immediately after the bridge, and after a few yards, you can rent a boat. Sail between icebergs, reach the foot of the largest glacier in Iceland whose name is difficult to pronounce the first time: Vatnajokulsthjodgardur.

To get on the black volcanic sand beach, just over the bridge, turn to the right. (Diamond, crystal, adamant Beach)

After walking on the South Coast, drive another 50 miles East to the town of Hofn. Stay here for the night.

Day three.

From Hofn to Egilsstadir with a stop in Stokksnes and Hengifoss. (130 miles in transit).

10 miles East of Hofn is the beautiful black beach of Stokksnes; to get to the beach, traveling 7 miles after Hofn, turn from the main road no. 1 to the right and go a couple of miles. You're at the right place.

After that, head north to Egilsstadir (120 miles), this is a very scenic spot, the largest fjord in the island's interior is located here.

If you want to walk on foot to places untouched by man, drive 20 miles inland to Hengifoss; you will see a spectacular gorge, the origins of the fjord and pristine nature.

After this nature walk, you will have strength only for going to sleep in Egilsstadir.

Day four.

From Egilsstadir to Akureyri with a view of Lake Myvatn, Dettifoss and Godafoss Waterfalls (215 miles in transit).

Continue to travel to the north of the island, going 100 miles to the largest waterfall, Dettifoss. An exciting experience is guaranteed.

After admiring the falls, continue your journey; go 50 miles in the direction of Akureyri and stop at the wonderful Lake Myvatn. You are in the geothermal area of Namaskard;

there are many mud baths. Make a circle around the lake, along the way you will be able to walk on the frozen lava.

Continue your way north about 30 miles after Lake Myvatn; turn left from the main road to see the waterfall Godafoss.

After such an eventful day trip you will drive another 35 miles to stay overnight in the Akureyri area.

Day five.

Sail through the fjords at Akureyri, traveling the North Coast, with a stop in Saudarkrokur.

Eat a good breakfast and head to the Eyjafjordur Fjord, at the mouth of Akureyri.

Here you can rent a boat with an experienced captain and go whale watching. Typically, these tours last up to three hours.

After the tour, drive along the North Coast and enjoy the beauty of the northern fjords. Leaving Akureyri from the west take Road 82 and continue on the Road 76. You will find 100 miles of beautiful scenic places in the north of Iceland.

Finish your day trip staying in the village of Saudarkrokur.

Day six.

From Saudarkrokur to Reykjavík with a view the Deildartunguhver geothermal source, historical place Reykholt, Hraunfossar and Barnafoss Waterfalls (225 miles in transit).

Leave early and drive towards Reykjavik. The first stop will be nearly 135 miles through the most powerful geothermal spring in Europe Deildartunguhver. This place is recognized was one of the best places to stay in 2016.

4 miles west of Deildartunguhver is located the historical place of Reykholt. In this place was the seam of the American and Eurasian tectonic plates.

Then continue the journey inland to the west for another 10 miles. You will come to two wonderful waterfalls, Hraunfossar and Barnafoss. These waterfalls are spewing huge amounts of water from fields of lava. It is an unbelievable sight.

After that, head to the end point of this trip to the capital, Reykjavik. The distance from here to Reykjavik is 75 miles.

On arrival in Reykjavik, this trip is over; you can relax in the capital and go elsewhere for new experiences.

CHAPTER 7 Helpful information for tourists

The official exchange rate is $1 approximately to 100–125 ISK www.cb.is

Visa information

Iceland is a party to the Schengen Agreement. This means that U.S. citizens may enter Iceland without a visa for up to 90 days for tourist or business purposes.

Your passport should be valid for at least three months beyond your intended date of departure from the Schengen area.

You need sufficient funds and a return airline ticket.

If your passport does not meet the Schengen requirements, you may be refused to board by the airline at your point of origin or while transferring planes. You could also be denied entry when you arrive in the Schengen area. For this reason, we recommend that your passport has at least six months' validity remaining whenever you travel abroad.

If necessary, you can always find support at the US Embassy in Iceland https://is.usembassy.gov

Useful phone numbers

Emergency number 112

Police 444-2500 (with country code +354-444-2500)

Medical assistance 1770

Dental emergency 575-0505

Directory inquiries 1818, 1819 or 1800

Mobile & internet in Iceland

Iceland GSM services (Siminn, Vodafone, TAL and Nova) cover most of the island, including a large proportion of the unpopulated area of the country. You can always easily buy a prepaid service (phone cards) from any of these GSM operators. At most gas stations or stores in Iceland you can purchase credit refill cards.

Also, you can rent a portable WiFi mobile internet hotspot and be connected to the internet anywhere in Iceland.

Unlimited 4G for 10$ a day https://iceland.trawire.com

How to call to Iceland from abroad. Dial:

Landline: **011** (Exit code for the USA) **354** (Iceland Code) **4 or 5** (Area Code) **- receiver number**

Cellular: **011** (Exit code for the USA) **354** (Iceland Code) **7 Digits Cellular Number**

Iceland area codes usually have 1 digits.

Area Name: *Reykjavik, Area code: 5*

Area Name: *outside Reykjavik, Area code: 4*

Also, calls can be made by dialing 00 next to the country code and next to the telephone number you wish to reach.

Save Your Budget in Iceland

Iceland is a civilized European country, environmentally pure, with a high level of service and comfort, low crime rate, homogeneous original population and a small amount of immigrants of the modern wave. However, you will hardly call your trip to Iceland budgetary. High taxes are imposed in the country, which affects prices of groceries, services, gas, etc.

Nevertheless, there is a possibility of optimizing your expenses in Iceland. To have a better idea how to do that, read tips on which way and on what things you can save your budget in Iceland.

1. Excursions. Do not use the services of intermediaries and book tours directly from local tour operators.

Apart from excursions, tourists are offered different types of active leisure, such as sailing, to watch whales and birds, descent into a volcanic chimney, fishing, riding horses, dog sleds, quad bikes, helicopter flights, diving, ice caps hiking, rafting, etc.

To avoid extra payments, book your tours and active leisure services directly from Icelandic tour operators, separate from package tours.

2. Hotels, apartments. Choose self-catering accommodation. Independently cooking breakfasts and dinners will help you to essentially save your budget. The perfect choice is apartment rental. Firstly, you'll have an equipped kitchen at your disposal and, secondly, the apartment will be considerably larger than a hotel room.

3. Food and water. Prices in cafes and restaurants are rather high in Iceland, especially at touristy places. A plate of meat soup + bread and butter will cost about 14 EUR, hot main course (meat or fish) 20–35 EUR, cup of coffee (tea) from 3 EUR and higher.

Groceries and non-alcohol beverages are sold at reasonable prices in the chain supermarkets Kronan and Bonus. These stores are available even at the historical center of Reykjavik and on Central Street, Laugavegur. Independent cooking of breakfast and dinner and sandwiches to have for lunch at excursions will help you to essentially save your money.

Also, it is useful to know that each cold water tap in Reykjavik and all over Iceland will provide you with absolutely pure drinking water, ready to use, not needing any boiling. Use this opportunity, pour cold tap water and drink it for free.

4. Clothing and footwear. Traveling to Iceland, a country with a northern climate and changing weather, you'll need to be well dressed and booted. Have a strong view on that. If you feel cold and uncomfortable, it will affect both your health and travel experiences. Cold rain and the wind (which is quite usual weather even in the summer) will simply make you go shopping to warm yourself up, and the prices for clothes, and especially footwear, are high in Iceland. To avoid extra expenses, think of taking warm clothes and shoes on your trip before leaving home.

Photo Survey of Some Icelandic Waterfalls

At the end of this book, I would like to introduce you to the beauty of the Icelandic waterfalls. I have prepared for you a list of the best waterfalls on the island with brief descriptions of each. I marked the location of the waterfalls with a star.

Aldeyjarfoss Waterfall

It seems that it is not worth a visit to Aldeyjarfoss because it is very far from the main routes of the tourists. But when you see the power of sparkling water masses whipping the ancient basalt columns and lava falling on the plains, you will understand that it is worth it.

Melted in the fire, the black plate with the icy stones looks dramatic.

Aldeyjarfoss waterfall

Dynjandi waterfall "Thunderous."

Dynjandi Waterfall is very picturesque in the west of Iceland.

It is a trapezoidal waterfall, the upper base of a giant "trapezoid"—100 feet, the bottom base is 200 feet. In fact,

Dynjandi connects seven small waterfalls with a total height of as much as 330 feet. Each of the seven waterfalls has a name: Fjallfoss, Hundafoss, Bæjarfoss, Hæstajallafoss, Hrísvaðsfoss, Strompgljúfrafoss, Göngumannafoss. There are stairs on the Dynjandi slopes.

Europe's most powerful waterfall is **Dettifoss**.

It instantly impresses with its size and the power of falling water.

Dettifoss waterfall.

The wild and violent waterfall is in the glacial river Jokulsá á Fjollum, in a national park in the northeast of the country, near Lake Myvatn.

Canyons along the river are often compared with the Great American canyons.

More than 130,000 gallons of water per second fall from a height of 145 feet, the width of the falls is 330 feet.

This raging monster is white in color as the waterfall is fed by water from the glacier with chalky sediments.

Fagrifoss Waterfall

This is an exciting waterfall in the center of the country, close to the Laki Volcano. Waterfall Fagrifoss is different from the other waterfalls. At the outset, waterfall shores are quite shallow and deepen very quickly. Travelers are not recommended to walk on the lower tiers. You could break away from the steep slope and fall into the swirling vortex.

Fagrifoss waterfall

Gullfoss Waterfall

Gullfoss waterfall

In Iceland, is the very famous two-tiered Gullfoss Waterfall. The upper tier of the falls is 36 feet, and the lower is 70 feet. The peculiarity of this waterfall is the constant fog here.

Usually, to see Gullfoss, tourists come from Reykjavik and it is included in the Golden List of Attractions, which are easy to see during the day.

Godafoss Waterfall

Godafoss waterfall

The River Skjalfandafljot falls down 40 feet and forms the majestic Waterfall Godafoss. This waterfall is located in the north of Iceland. It was called "Waterfall of God" because a law speaker, Thorgeir Ljosvetningagodi Thorkelsson made Christianity the official religion of Iceland in the year 1000. The Godafoss Waterfall is so popular that a lot of tourists come to see it from near and far.

Glymur Waterfall, "Flickering."

The highest waterfall in Iceland is Glymur.

This waterfall is taller than the pyramid of ancient Egyptian Pharaoh Cheops. Glymur's altitude is 650 feet.

It is a tiered waterfall, and the natural arch stretches one of the first steps.

Near Glymur are many caves, through which guided tours can be enjoyed.

Glymur waterfall

In the old days, to get to the east of the fjord of Hvalfordure, people had to cross 'the waterfall. But now there is a new, reliable tunnel under the fjord. No one is walking the old trails. Locals say it is extremely dangerous.

Hraunfossar Waterfall

The amazing waterfall Hraunfossar was formed by the confluence of many streams. The name of the waterfall translates from Icelandic as "falling of lava".

In fact, Hraunfossar is born from the lava flow, and there are about 900 natural springs. This water streamed over the deep ruts and grooves in the lava. To photograph the entire waterfall is tough, but each part is worthy of your attention. Near the waterfall there are a lot of north soft flowers and they are beautiful.

Hjalparfoss Waterfall

Hjalparfoss waterfall

Hjalparfoss is great double-tiered waterfall near the confluence of Rivers Thjorsa and Fossa in the Thjorsa Valley. "Falling Help" is the translation of the name of the aterfall. The surrounding area is called Hjalp (Help). The legend tells about the first settlers who came to this place. They were drained and found great help in this growing area to graze their horses after a long trip. Locals say this waterfall is delicious and has almost healing water.

Oxararfoss Waterfall

Oxararfoss waterfall

This mysterious waterfall is a UNESCO heritage site and located in the south of Iceland. People believe that this waterfall on the river Oxara was created artificially, a few centuries ago, for the purpose of water intake. In winter, the lower part of Oxararfoss freezes and bubbling jets fall on the ice blocks, it looks fantastic. This waterfall is located exactly in the geological border of the Eurasian and the North American continental plates. Oxararfoss is located 35 miles from Reykjavik.

Svartifoss Waterfall

Svartifoss waterfall

Svartifoss is a beautiful waterfall due to the massive basalt columns that rise at its sides. You can see the columns up close, they look human-made, but this is a creation of

Mother Nature. The name of the waterfall translates as "the fall of the dark", and these water masses among the black columns attract travelers from around the world. The waterfall is about 70 feet.

Seljalandsfoss Waterfall

Seljalandsfoss waterfall

The glacial River Seljalandsa flows in the southwest of Iceland. The powerful, tall, narrow, beautiful Seljalandsfoss Waterfall is a decoration of this river. Seljalandsfoss is about 200 feet tall. This waterfall is easy to see. You do not need to move from the main central ring road of Iceland. Some climbers will make the risky climb on the slippery rocks, however.

Selfoss Waterfall

Selfoss is one of four waterfalls on the River Jokulsá á Fjollum (Dettifoss Waterfall is on this river). It is wide and extends for 350 feet, but the height is only 36 feet. Selfoss

Waterfall is enormous and, of course, an excellently beautiful landmark. Along the banks there are organized trips for fans to take pictures. If you go down the river, you'll find the Waterfall Dettifoss.

Thjofafoss Waterfall

Thjofafoss waterfall

In the southern region of Iceland, crossing the volcanic plateau is the flowing Thjorsa River. On this river, there are many waterfalls. The most beautiful of them is the waterfall of Thjófafoss. The name translates as "a fall of robbers". According to legend, there were drowned criminals in this river. The water cascades down from the black rocks in the roaring whirlpools. It looks almost unearthly, like a computer illustration of a fantastic film.

Dear readers, thanks for reading my book. I hope you found something interesting to learn. If you do not like something, please send me an email larskkjonsson@gmail.com and we can talk about it. I'm glad to meet with my readers. I'm writing for you, and I want to do it better.

I am always working on improving my books. When I publish the updates, or for example photo albums, I will send you the updated books to your e-mail.

Thanks!
Sincerely for you,
Lars K. Jonsson

Disclaimer and Terms of Use: Effort has been made to ensure that the information in this book is accurate and complete. However, the author and the publisher do not warrant the accuracy of the information, text and graphics contained within the book due to the rapidly changing nature of science, research, known and unknown facts and internet. The Author and the publisher do not hold any responsibility for errors, omissions or contrary interpretation of the subject matter herein. This book is presented solely for motivational and informational purposes only.

Made in the USA
Middletown, DE
06 January 2018